What people are saying about *Advertising Without an Agency Made Easy*

"*Advertising Without an Agency* provides the knowledge you need to make informed decisions about spending your advertising dollars to produce results. This is an excellent resource for anyone starting a business."
> —Vada Penner, Administrator
> Canadian Women's Business Network

"This is exactly the kind of information I needed when I started my business. It would have saved me years of frustration trying to learn it myself."
> —Barry Edwards
> United States SBA Louisiana Small
> Business Person of the Year 2000

"Kathy Kobliski has put together a book offering some good street savvy information for business owners to use in building their marketing model. *Advertising Without an Agency Made Easy* is a robust and well-rounded book of information."
> —Gene Fairbrother
> MBA Consulting, Inc.

"The book is not only right on target, but an absolute must-read for all small business owners. Over the years I have read every book on advertising that I could get my hands on, and this one is clearly the best I have ever read."
> —Bob Anderson
> United States SBA Oregon Small Business
> Person of the Year 2004

Additional titles in Entrepreneur's Made Easy Series

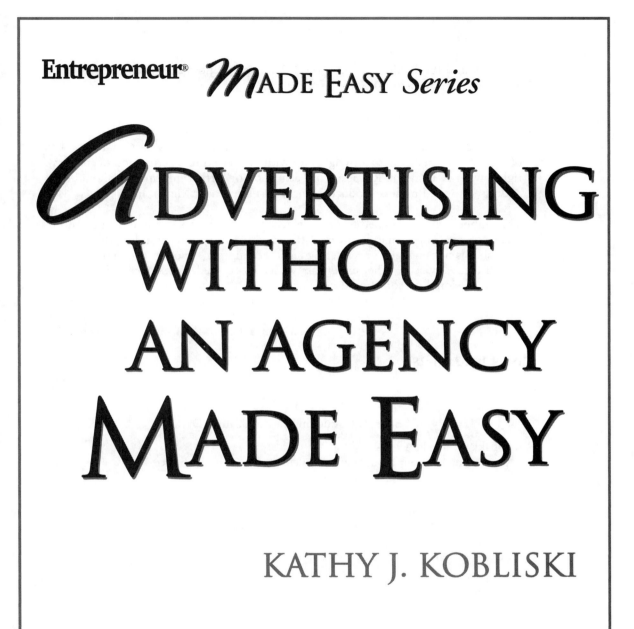

Entrepreneur® MADE EASY Series

ADVERTISING WITHOUT AN AGENCY MADE EASY

KATHY J. KOBLISKI

EP Entrepreneur® Press

Editorial Director: Jere Calmes
Cover Design: Beth Hanson-Winter
Editorial and Production Services: CWL Publishing Enterprises, Inc., Madison,
Wisconsin, www.cwlpub.com

This publication is designed to provide accurate and authoritative information in
regard to the subject matter covered. It is sold with the understanding that the
publisher is not engaged in rendering legal, accounting, or other professional services. If legal advice or other expert assistance is required, the services of a competent professional person should be sought.
—From a Declaration of Principles jointly adopted by
a Committee of the American Bar Association and
a Committee of Publishers and Associations

ISBN 1-932531-28-9

Library of Congress Cataloging-in-Publication Data
Kobliski, Kathy J., 1946-
  Advertising without an agency made easy / by Kathy Kobliski.
    p. cm. — (Entrepreneur made easy series)
  Includes index.
  ISBN 1-932531-28-9
    1. Advertising. 2. Small business. I. Title. II. Series.
  HF5823.K624 2005
  659.1—dc22

                                                            2005040014

Printed in Canada

10 09 08 07 06 05   10 9 8 7 6 5 4 3 2

Contents

Contents

Dedication

To my husband Frank, with love

Preface

ADVERTISING IS THE ART OF LETTING PEOPLE KNOW YOU ARE OPEN and interested in having their business. Failing to advertise is planning to keep your business a secret.

Advertising is not a perfect science. It's not even close. It can be frustrating, confusing, expensive, and sometimes overwhelming, and too time-consuming for the small business owner who has so many other responsibilities. Thousands of dollars can easily be wasted by making uninformed advertising decisions. Your entire business can be lost by deciding not to advertise at all.

There are so many kinds of advertising from which to choose. Since you are not a professional media buyer, how are you supposed to know what would work best for your business? How do you make informed decisions independently from what you are told by the media sales reps who call on you every day? Which of those media reps do you believe? There may be no other facet of your business in which so many friendly people can so easily lead you astray. How do you know which radio and television stations are the best ones to use? Which publications and billboards will increase the demand for your product or service?

I designed this book to help you avoid common mistakes and provide timesaving, energy-saving, money-saving information. It is not for the advertising experts who can chew up and spit out information from Arbitron and Nielsen over breakfast. They don't need my help. But it is for the direct advertiser who must keep up with changing formats and audiences of radio stations, shifting television lineups, special sections of various publications, as well as the stories and "numbers" recited by media sales people—all while trying to meet the many other daily demands of running a business. It is for the small business owner who understands the importance of advertising and is stuck doing it alone.

- ▶ Radio is the "Theater of the Mind," but you can lose sleep wondering if anyone is listening to the station playing your ad for those particular seconds.
- ▶ Television provides sound and movement, but how much of your message actually survives the zappers? And how do you choose from the gazillions of stations out there?
- ▶ Outdoor advertising works for you from dawn to dusk. But don't the same people drive by day in and day out?
- ▶ Print is historically a staple of advertising, but is circulation going down? Do people read the paper from cover to cover these days or do they get their news from TV and radio? How many people will actually read the page your ad is on?
- ▶ Direct mail can blanket entire or specific communities. But do people read fliers and inserts or do they think of them as junk mail?
- ▶ Yellow Pages advertising lends credibility to your business. But do you want to be jammed on a page with all of your competitors? Do you want your expensive ad leading consumers to your competitors who not only share the page but also may have a larger ad?
- ▶ The Internet is still new and still confusing. It's difficult to tell how well banner ads and click-throughs work—or if they're working at all. How do you get people to visit your web site? And how the heck do you keep them coming back?

I wrote this book to take some of the mystery out of the advertising process, arm you with material to remove much of the guesswork and frustration you may have experienced in the past, and allow you to work those advertising dollars harder than ever to grow your business.

Remember that advertising's only job is to make that phone ring, increase traffic in your store, and generate interest in your product or service. Once your advertising has achieved that response, it's up to you to come through with friendly, helpful, knowledgeable employees, effective follow-through on sales or service, and all of the other aspects that go into maintaining consumer or client interest that your advertising has generated.

A friend once told me that trying to attract customers without advertising is like winking at someone in the dark. You're the only one who knows what you're doing and you're never going to get any results. So, the next time advertising comes up—and you know it will—grab this book instead of an antacid tablet and create an affordable, successful plan for a week or a year!

Introduction

GET THE BUSINESS OPEN AND WORRY ABOUT ADVERTISING LATER. This is the unfortunate inclination of many prospective and functioning small business owners—unfortunate because it relegates to the back burner the critical, final step of connecting their businesses and their prospects.

Liken it to a high school student who does homework but doesn't turn it in. Or a baker who fills a cake pan with batter but doesn't put it into the oven. Or a bookkeeper who prepares invoices but doesn't mail them out. Or to any employee who works all week and fails to cash his or her paycheck. These final steps are what trigger the big payoffs—to skip them would be ludicrous.

During my 25 years in the field of advertising, I have constantly run across small business owners who resist advertising like the plague… even though it is the final, critical step in the success of a business. Without it there is no payoff—just like there is no credit for homework done but not turned it, no cake without putting the batter into the oven, no receivables for invoices not mailed, and no money to pay the rent for the worker who fails to cash a paycheck.

Yes, advertising is expensive. But so are the computers, scanners, desks, chairs, phones, copy machines, registers, inventory, and delivery vehicles needed to set up a business. Financial provisions are always made for those essentials: no one plans to scrounge at the local landfill to get business machines and inventory for free. A dollar figure is always allowed for payroll, because people won't come to work every day out of the goodness of their hearts. An amount of money for rent and utilities is put aside; obviously one cannot set up a business in an abandoned garage and use lanterns for light and maybe build a campfire for warmth. So why, when it comes to advertising, *the very link between a business and its custom*ers, do so many small business owners look for ways to get around it?

I've been asked hundreds of times how to advertise for free. Here's my answer: *you can't!* Not if you expect to see results that will build your business. Sure, an opportunity may come along now and then, but you should never, *never* count on that to do the serious work of brand-building or the task of familiarizing the public with the name of your business and your products or services. I'm not saying you shouldn't take advantage of the no-cost or low-cost ads when you can, but you have to consider those opportunities as *additions* to a continual paid advertising effort. Without promoting your location, the name of your business, and your products and services to the very people you want to show up, what do you think will happen? I can tell you. You'll go out of business and be stuck with a store full of equipment and inventory and lose your shirt.

I've said before that opening a business without advertising is like making elaborate plans for a huge party and then not sending out invitations. How the heck would the guests know where the party is? What day? What time? How would they even know that there is a party? What would happen then? The host would be standing in a room with lots of decorations, expensive food, and music ... alone. Neglect to send out invitations to your business, in the form of advertising, and you'll be alone in your store or office.

Advertising is a critical part of the success of any business, large or small. It cannot be avoided, overlooked, underestimated, undervalued, or dismissed. Do you have salespeople who need to go out and sell? It's certainly easier for them to do so when the potential customers are at least aware of the company and have a positive perception of it than when no one has ever heard of the business. Advertising provides credibility that will turn into cash! So avoid the mindset of *"I'll just get the business open now and worry about the advertising later."* When "later" comes and you realize that unlocking the door and turning on the lights aren't enough to bring in customers, here's what will happen:

▶ You'll realize that you must advertise after all.

▶ You'll start advertising, even though you don't have the cash "in hand" to pay for it, and hope that it will bring in enough business to pay for itself. That never happens.

▶ You'll have trouble paying for the ads you ran and earn yourself a "bad pay" reputation that will spread throughout the media in your market like a wildfire.

▶ You won't be able to get a decent rate during your next stab at advertising because you will not be negotiating from a position of strength. No one is going to give you a price break because you took so long to pay off your last invoices. In fact, you'll probably be relegated to a "cash in advance" status.

All this because you didn't include an advertising budget in your business plan. Does this sound like the part of your business that should be downgraded to an afterthought? The truth here is simple and I'm repeating myself for the hundredth time: if you have not made financial provisions to advertise your business right from the get-go, *you are simply not ready to open.*

I can't count the number of times over the years that I have seen small business owners pinch pennies on advertising while they're open, then spend like crazy to advertise their going-out-of-business sale. How can advertising be necessary to take the message to the public that a business is closing when it wasn't considered necessary enough to carry the message that the business was open?

Rocco Torres, Creative Director of Media Dimensions/E Factor Media, Inc. in San Diego, California *(www.efactormedia.com)*, advises,

> Many small businesses, when preparing their business plan, do not add in capital investment for promotion and/or advertising. Large advertising budgets are not required. Moderate investments, if used creatively, can go a long way. A solid business strategy would allocate 3-5 percent of company spending to advertising as an example. I would suggest hiring a marketing consultant before starting up the business to get some ideas on how to promote on a small budget. And look for other "small" businesses that offer graphic design services for a lower cost than a large agency.

A humble advertising budget forces you to find specific radio stations, television programs, daily and weekly publications, direct mail possibilities, and outdoor advertising that will create interest in your business and bring in the most customers. And now you also have to think of ways to drive people to your web site and keep them there! You are expected to achieve, in whatever amount of time you can squeeze out of your day, a specifically targeted advertising plan without wasting any of your precious advertising dollars in the process.

I can't count the number of times over the years that I have seen small business owners pinch pennies on advertising while they're open, then spend like crazy to advertise their going-out-of-business sale.

This is a full-time job for advertising executives. It takes knowledge of the market; the ability to read, dissect, and understand market indicators from Arbitron and Nielsen; the capacity to creatively attract the attention of audiences; and the discipline to meet deadlines, negotiate contracts, and quickly re-evaluate and sometimes revise strategies to deal with changes in the market. How are you supposed to do this in your spare time and do it as well as the pros?

I'm hoping that the fact that you're showing interest in this book means that you and I agree that you are going to have to advertise, ... that advertising really is the final necessary step in bringing your business and your customers together, ... that standing on the street corner and yelling to passersby won't make you successful.

Advertising without an agency is not like wallpapering your guest bathroom by yourself or landscaping your yard a little each year to save money. Once you start to advertise, every dollar counts and all aspects of the endeavor become critical.

The good news is that your media sales reps are, for the most part, knowledgeable professionals and the really great news is that you don't have to be. The information and the worksheets in this book will arm you with the facts that are necessary to place your advertising dollars where they will do the most good every time. You will learn how to use the various forms of media to grow your business, how to keep track of your decisions (and results) for future reference, and where to look for help with all of it.

Acknowledgments

MANY THANKS TO THE FOLLOWING COMMUNICATION AND advertising agencies, for graciously providing significant quotes and advertising samples throughout the book. Small business owners will find these generous contributions from experienced and accomplished experts invaluable. In alphabetical order:

AdPotential—Mount Kisco, New York

Cactus Marketing Communications—Denver, Colorado

Creative Producers Group, Inc.—St. Louis, Missouri

BBDO—Atlanta, Georgia

E Factor Media, Inc.—San Diego, California

Epicenter Advertising—San Diego, California

Gelphman Associates—San Jose, California

Gravity Metrics—Denver, Colorado

GTK Marketing Group—Brooklyn, New York

Guy Lyman Advertising—Dallas, Texas

Hodge Communications—Chicago, Illinois

Lamar Outdoor Advertising—Syracuse, New York

Leap Frog Advertising—New York, New York

Logosharx Logo Design—Sparta, Wisconsin

McLaughlin & Morgan—Philadelphia, Pennsylvania

MCM Communications—Harrison, New York

Mercury Radio Research—San Diego, California

MRW Communications—Boston, Massachusetts

Obie Media—Eugene, Oregon

Off Madison Ave—Tempe, Arizona

PageWorks Communication Design—Denver, Colorado

Partners & Levit Advertising—New York, New York

Reasons Group. Inc.—Dallas/Fort Worth, Texas

Risdall Advertising—St. Paul, Minnesota

Robert Brandt & Associates—Chicago, Illinois

Robert Smith & Associates PR—Rockton, Illinois

Roska Direct—Philadelphia, Pennsylvania

Sterling-Rice Group—Boulder, Colorado

The BrainStorm Group—Toronto, Canada

The Republik—Durham, North Carolina

Think Factory—Miami, Florida

Time Warner—Syracuse, New York

ToTheWeb, LLC—San Mateo, California

Warne/McKenna Advertising—Syracuse, New York

Wordsworth & Company, LLC—Santa Monica, California

And my thanks to the following professionals who made important contributions to this book:

Rob Frankel, consultant and author

Shel Horowitz, author

Sharon Senter, marketing consultant

Chapter 1

Define Your
Business

B EFORE YOU CAN NAME YOUR BUSINESS, DESCRIBE IT, AND PROMOTE IT to the public, you must completely understand what it's all about yourself. You have to be able to write it out on paper in an organized, succinct manner.

What is the nature of your business? What is the purpose of the business? What are the goals of your business? Creating a mission statement—simmering down all the ingredients that define your product(s) and service(s) into a few written sentences—is a good way to start and should lead you to the core of your advertising message.

Your mission statement may include personal or industrial convictions. It may contain a lengthier explanation of what you want your business to mean to the community or the world. You may want to develop two mission statements—one internal and one external. An internal statement can give you and your employees a reason to get up in the morning, like the famous mission statement from Nike, "Crush Reebok," or Pepsi's "Beat Coke" or Honda's "We will crush, squash, and slaughter Yamaha." These are great to get your juices flowing every day—but you should perhaps think about something different for the public.

Whatever you choose as your mission statement, the exercise of figuring it out will force you to put a lot of thought into your business, the way you will run it, how you regard your customers, the importance you place on your business reputation, and the corporate "feeling" you want to convey to the public. And what will you call your new business?

What's in a name? "Pretty much everything," says Ritchie Lucas, founder and CEO of Think Factory in Miami, Florida (*www.thinkfactory.com*):

> The time and creative energy spent on your company name can be the most cost-effective time you can spend. It's enduring and powerful. It's the cover of your book and the sign of your life. It's the difference between getting someone's attention at the first hello or just being passed by. A great corporate name says what you are and why you do what you do.
>
> However, there is a catch. You must be able to pull it off. Your name should not only reflect a lot about what you do, but it should be representative of your company's personality. In a time when company culture has become as important as the work, the name can get you in the door. We're all consumers. Take a second to think what names pique your interest or cause you to at least pick up a phone or stop into a store. With all things considered equal, a great name can be the intangible that gets you the business.

Get a Logo

Your logo will appear on your business cards, letterhead, envelopes, contracts, packaging, and web site. It will give definition and identity to your business.

After naming your business, designing your business logo is one of the first things you do. It will appear on your business cards, letterhead, envelopes, contracts, packaging, and web site. It will give definition and identity to your business in terms of formal vs. informal, conservative vs. colorful, serious vs. humorous. As a small or new business, you may not have the funds to hire a graphic artist to develop a logo, but expensive graphics are not necessary to create an identifying look for your business. Look in the Yellow Pages of your local phone book for a typesetter or printer. They will help you select fonts (styles of lettering), shading, color, and any number of other options to create your own special look.

Kelly Dailey, Creative Director of Logosharx Logo Design in Sparta, WI (*www.logosharx.com*), sends us the logo samples shown in Figure 1-1.

Your letterhead, business cards, merchandise bags, and ads define your business to your customers. Be sure they say what you want them to, what you intend them to, right from the start.

Everything should carry the same colors, fonts, and slogan. The Internet

Figure 1-1. Logo examples

is the place to repeat and enhance all of it, since you can use text, photos, animation, and sound on your web site. It's all part and parcel of your advertising efforts. Every component ties together and reflects all of the other elements in every way.

Try different combinations until you find a design that's visually pleasing and projects an accurate impression of your business. You can find clip art books and computer software in almost any store carrying business or art supplies. If you would like more than distinctive lettering as part of your logo, use artwork found in these sources to add some extra interest. Clip art is available on the Internet—just do a search for "clip art" with any search engine—but be careful that you don't achieve a "cartoon" look. You also run the risk of using clip art that someone else in your area has used. You want your look to be unique.

A good piece of advice comes from Rosemary Brisco, President of ToTheWeb (*www.totheweb.com*) of San Mateo, California.

> It's impossible to place a dollar value on professional presentation materials such as business cards, brochures, or a web site. It can often make the difference between a customer selecting you or one of your competitors. Looking like a pro helps justify higher prices. Work with a designer to carry your corporate image across all your materials.

Your business logo will become more and more recognizable as time goes on—especially if you've put a lot of thought into making it unique.

TIP: For formal letterhead, envelopes, and business cards, use a more expensive paper and card stock. But for informal communications and invoices, use simple, less expensive paper and envelopes to save some money.

There should never be an envelope, piece of letterhead, Yellow Page ad, print ad, outdoor billboard, contract, invoice, or merchandise bag that leaves your company without your logo on it.

Push it further and consider using your logo colors to paint the outside of your door and around your windows or have your logo etched into the glass portion of your door if you're within a business complex. The more it's seen, the faster it will become recognizable.

You want a logo that will stand out in an ad, a pile of mail, a pile of invoices, or a pile of business cards. Consider how recognizable the unlikely Gateway Computer color scheme is.

There is nothing more boring and less inspiring than a business card with a few lines of black print on a white background. Even the most buttoned-down, laid-back, let's say, accounting firm (sorry!) can have a handsome (but not creative—a word accounting firms probably don't want to be associated with), dignified, interesting logo.

Ask your printer for samples of other business cards. They will have hundreds to show you. Look at and feel different stocks and weights of paper to find the one you want. After all, when you hand out a business card, it may be the only tangible reminder the person has of you and your business for days, weeks, or months after your meeting. Make it memorable! If you are not particularly good at or interested in design and color combinations, ask a friend or family member who has some talent to help make choices.

Rolodex cards made up with your business name on the tab are easy to file and make it simple for that customer or client to find your phone, fax, URL, and e-mail numbers in a hurry. The easier you make it for people to find you and do business with you, the more successful you will be.

Issue a Press Release

One of the first things you want to do is make a public announcement, in the form of a press release, that your business exists and is open. This may be the first time anyone has the opportunity to learn about your business and you want to make a good impression on the readers.

Very few local publications will print a press release just because you write it and send it in. OK, so maybe they are not as excited as you are about your new endeavor. Find an angle that will make them interested.

Once you are certain that the information is indeed newsworthy, a good heading is a great place to start. If you study the regular articles in your daily or weekly papers, you'll see that the titles of the articles are written to attract the readers' attention. You need to make their job easy: if they have to work to pull interesting or relevant facts from your piece, they won't bother. Stick to the facts.

Get the good stuff out up front—in the first ten to 12 words if possible. Don't use a lot of adjectives. Edit harshly. If you can't do it, have someone else edit it for you. Provide your contact information:

▶ Phone and fax numbers

▶ Address

▶ URL

▶ E-mail address

Use some creativity to get people interested. Look for an interesting angle, an offbeat, comical, or ironic twist. Create your press release with the readers in mind. Make it short, interesting, and above all, give it a catchy title. If you stick to this plan you'll have a better chance of seeing your press release in print.

Shel Horowitz, author of *Principled Profit: Marketing That Puts People First* and *Grassroots Marketing: Getting Noticed in a Noisy World* (*www.frugalmarketing.com*), says,

> I was hired to write a press release for a new book on electronic privacy. Instead of the boring, expected "Electronic Privacy Expert Releases New Book," my headline was "It's 10 O'clock—Do You Know Where Your Credit History Is?"
>
> As for press kits, don't waste money on fancy folders. Most of my press kits are e-mailed, faxed, or downloaded from one of my web sites. Include some or all of these in yours:
>
> ▶ Press releases
> ▶ Bio
> ▶ Company background
> ▶ Clips of other coverage/list of media appearances
> ▶ Suggested interview questions (may be different for print, radio, or TV)
> ▶ Product sample(s)
>
> Include your contact information, including e-mail, web address, and phone on every page.

Many weekly community papers have a feature called "Business of the Week" or "Business Person of the Week." You'll have an easier time getting into that feature—at least in the edition that covers your geographic area—

if you do a little paid advertising in the publication now and again. Call the editor and ask him or her to consider you for the feature. Provide a photo of you inside or in front of your location. Put together some black-and-white photos, as well as color, for different opportunities that come along.

Take Stock When Defining Your Business— Can You Diversify?

You may be able to increase your customer base and cash flow if you can widen the definition of your business.

You may be able to increase your customer base and cash flow if you can widen the definition of your business. Ask yourself if there is another branch you can add to your business tree. Diversifying your business from a single-purpose operation can not only bring in supplemental operating cash, but it can save your business when times get tough for your main business or when the economic environment is generally poor.

▶ If you own a store that sells musical instruments and accessories, you could give music lessons and do repairs or collect rare instruments and sell them on the Internet. Perhaps set up a small studio where local musicians can come to cut demos or rent space for local bands to rehearse. Think of all the parents who would gladly pay not to have that noise in their garage or basement.

▶ If you own an antique furniture store that also sells art and collectibles from different periods, you could rent such items to local theater groups for authentic stage props or to television stations for commercial settings. (Check your insurance and theirs!) Refinishing classes on the weekends or classes on identifying antiques at garage and tag sales would probably be well attended. You may even be able to organize a bus trip to a neighboring state known for its antiques.

▶ If you own a bakery, you could tie your cakes into family restaurants that provide children's birthday parties or your donuts and pastries into restaurants serving breakfast. You could hold classes on cake decorating, wedding etiquette, and even wedding fashion shows to bolster the wedding cake portion of the business. If you have the space, you can turn it into a decorated "for rent" birthday party room. You can cater as much of the food as you want—just the cakes, breads, and your daily fare or all of the food.

▶ If you're a florist, you could hold classes on flower arranging, sponsor a bridal show, and approach local restaurants and hotels for providing weekly arrangements for tables, lobbies, or for special events like conventions.

There are many ways to use your knowledge to branch out from your main business and make it pay. Hold instructional or informational classes, special shows, demonstrations, collector events. Make use of extra space. Write a "how-to" book .... Put on your thinking cap! It's possible the diversification could end up being your biggest moneymaker and become your primary business in the future.

Check the Yellow Pages display ads of your competitors. See what products or services they highlight. Do you see any diversification going on there? Pay attention to their radio and television commercials, outdoor billboards, and print ads. Learn from people in your business who have been around and successful for a long time.

While you're looking at your competitors' ads, think about what products you have or services you can provide that your competitors cannot. Ask yourself why someone should seek you out, as opposed to going to one of your competitors.

You must have a reason or you are in trouble right from the beginning. Just to tell the public, "Hey, here's one more book store, one more shoe store, one more restaurant," is not going to make them check you out. People are creatures of habit and unless you give them something new, exciting, different, better priced, of higher quality, etc., they will go where they are used to going for their goods and services. What is your special niche? What's special about your business that makes it worth someone's while to pass by your competitors and walk through your door?

Scrutinize!

Give yourself an honest evaluation of what your business looks like today—where it should be, where it has to go. You can check each area of your business (sales, management, customer service, purchasing, products, accounting, etc.) with a SWOT analysis.

Using SWOT analysis worksheet (Figure 1-2) will define your strengths, weaknesses, opportunities, and threats and set you off on the right path. Make a copy of the following chart for each area of your business.

Then, start by listing your personal and business *strengths* and *weaknesses*. These are internal and will spell out where the muscle is that makes your business competitive and define the areas in which you need to

7

improve. Seeing your weaknesses on paper will give you a chance to determine how to fortify those areas.

The last two categories, *opportunities* and *threats*, are external forces, again one good and one bad. List the opportunities that you have or will have for improving your business and describe how you plan to seize each opportunity. List the threats that can keep you from growing, excelling, and taking advantages of the opportunities you listed. Determine the best way to go around, over, under, or through or to avoid these obstacles all together. This is an important look at what's going on in the marketplace that can affect your business.

A great example of this is what's happened to Krispy Kreme, which purchased Montana Mills Bread Co., a bakery/restaurant chain, in January 2003 to diversify its operations. The increased popularity of low-carb diets took bread and donuts off the lists of many consumers. In May 2004, Krispy Kreme discontinued operations of its Montana Mills line.

You'll need more than one SWOT analysis. The first is just the beginning. It will lead you to a point in time when all four categories will have changed in some way and you can put another one together. It's a great organizational tool to keep you from losing focus. Include on this form facts about employees, management, finances, office policies, return and customer service policies, etc., as well as about your products and services.

Once you have truly defined your business, named it, decided on a logo, and explored possible ways to diversify, be it with classes, writings, workshops, or creating on-line business, you're ready to move forward. Your job now is to define your market.

This is one of the most important steps you will take in structuring your advertising plans. Why? Because if you are not sure who your customers are, you will not be able to make sound advertising decisions and all of the work you've done thus far won't matter.

This is truly a step-by-step procedure that all entrepreneurs should follow. To leave out any one part is the same as leaving out an essential ingredient in a recipe.

Take a deep breath and go on to the next chapter!

SWOT WORKSHEET	
Strengths	**Weaknesses**
What efforts will you make to keep them? _____ _____ _____	What efforts will you make to strengthen them? _____ _____ _____
Opportunities	**Threats**
How will you take advantage of them? _____ _____ _____	How will you overcome them? _____ _____ _____

Figure 1-2. SWOT analysis worksheet—fill in the four categories and actions for each

Chapter 2

Develop Your Brand

ALL THROUGH YOUR BUSINESS LIFE, YOU WILL TRY TO BUILD AND control the mental image that your company name evokes, and how the public perceives the business. The current term for this is *branding*, but it's really only a combination of the things people have always needed to do to build and maintain a successful business. Decide in what light you want the public to see your business and then determine what you need to do to get there.

Ron Telpner, Chairman and CEO of The BrainStorm Group in Toronto, Canada (*www.brainstormgroup.com*), says that branding isn't everything, but without it, there's nothing else.

> I am a big believer in branding. And branding means using every channel available to get the message out. But not just any message. I call this marrying commerce with creativity. It all starts with understanding the DNA of the brand, where it fits in the hearts and minds of the customer, what problem it solves, and what is its relevant differentiation. Once a brand is established and a connection is made with the customer, the great marketer will continue to refine and refocus. This is key because, once you have figured out what the customer wants, they change. The process is ongoing.

I came from a small market where ideas were big but budgets were small. It meant understanding integrated marketing and communication to get maximum impact with few dollars. The starting point was always the same because we had to answer a few simple questions: Who do you want to talk to? What do you want to tell them? What do they think of you now? What do you want them to think? Why should they believe you? Answer those questions and you are on your way to solving the problem.

Conducting brainstorm sessions is an excellent way to get great ideas on the table. We do this with new and existing clients on a regular basis. The result is the occasional big idea that makes a huge noise in the market. If you don't start with a sound idea that is on strategy, don't waste money on bad ads! Finally, for the small advertiser who can't really afford an agency, my advice is simple: if everyone zigs, you should zag!

Branding is the intangible, "goodwill" portion of your business, which has nothing to do with its location, real estate, or inventory. Instead, it refers to the company's good name, logo, and reputation. It's what creates loyalty in your current customers and provides familiarity and comfort to encourage new customers. It demands respect in the community and, if carefully tended, will be worth more in actual dollars than all of the tangible assets put together. Your brand is what will line your pockets when you're ready to sell your business down the road.

Robert Brandt, CEO of Robert Brandt & Associates in Chicago, Illinois (*www.robertbrandt.com*), advises,

Your most valuable asset is your brand. It's your future. Your brand is a promise, a totality, a reputation.

Robert Shaw West, Chairman/CEO of The Republik in Durham, North Carolina (*www.therepublik.net*), says,

People don't buy anything because of an ad. People buy brands. And a brand isn't created by any single effort, but rather a sequence of events—points of contact—that give your brand substance, meaning, and relevance to its prospect. Every interaction your brand has with its customers will ultimately determine its success. So make sure you carefully think through your salesperson interaction, how you handle a return, your answering machine recording, the look of your letterhead, the direct mail, your web site—and your ad.

Branding is the intangible, "goodwill" portion of your business, which has nothing to do with its location, real estate, or inventory.

11

What Influences Your Branding Efforts?

Customer Service

Your employees have a tremendous influence on branding. People are put off by salespeople who attack like a SWAT team as soon as they enter the store or employees who position themselves within three feet of customers and pretend to be busy, when it's obvious they're making sure the customer isn't going to steal something. Patrons who are treated rudely on the phone or on your sales floor will carry word-of-mouth criticism far and wide. Don't hire or keep employees who couldn't care less about your business. As a consumer, you've experienced employees who shrug their shoulders rather than help you find something, say they're too busy to check to see when a shipment you're waiting for is expected to arrive, or carry on a personal phone conversation while you wait at the counter. Get every employee on board with your branding efforts or get them out, even if they're related to you. It won't matter what kind of advertising you do to get people in the door and it won't matter how many come, if they're treated badly when they get there. They won't return—and they'll keep others away.

PR or "Buzz" Marketing

Tied into customer service in many ways, public relations also can add speed to your business branding. You may not be able to afford a famous spokesperson to sing your praises or a national "taste test" approach to educate the public about the quality of your products, but you can initiate some important, but low-cost steps locally to get started.

Rosemary Brisco from ToTheWeb tells us:

Promote your business on a 24/7 basis. The most cost-effective and most overlooked lead-generation tool is a referral. Tell your current clients and friends about the results you produce for your clients. For example, don't say, "We build web sites for businesses." Instead say, "We build web sites that increase sales leads by 50 percent." But don't exaggerate.

Your Willingness to Use the Web

The people in your market browse the net for information as much as for shopping and you want them to be able to access you there.

Maybe you are not interested in selling globally; perhaps you won't sell anything at all from your web site. You still need to have a web presence to show your clients that you are on top of things and using the newest technology. The people in your market browse the net for information as much as for shopping and you want them to be able to access you there. A web site is a great place to put a coupon that customers can print and use at your brick-and-mortar location or to offer a discount or product that's only available on your web site. And a URL on your business card, letterhead, contracts, invoices, and ads tells the public you're operating on all cylinders.

Your efforts to build your brand must be constantly tended over the years, as it needs to be expanded, changed, or even redeemed. Control what you can. Small breaches can be remedied and customer confidence can be reestablished. But restoring a severely broken brand is like trying to stop an elaborate maze of tumbling dominos.

Branding tells the story of your company. It's the perception of your company in the minds of your customers, employees, and suppliers. It's essential for growth, the bottom line, and increased perceived value. Starbucks is a good example of branding. Coffee at one time was just a warm beverage. Something that simple has become a lifestyle and cultural phenomenon through branding. Through image, product differentiation, and increased perceived value, a simple hot beverage has become a hot brand name.

Robert Gelphman, Principal of Gelphman Associates in San Jose, California (*www.gelphman.com*), says:

> Brand is an emotional appeal to a group or an individual's psyche, heart, and lifestyle. It is a promise of quality, trust, availability, and unwavering commitment to the product or service by the company. It is also time-consuming, expensive, and difficult to measure. Its underlying and only attribute is there is no risk to the purchase.
>
> What often goes wrong with marketing campaigns can be traced to a disconnect between branding and positioning. Too many VPs of marketing, their product managers, and their CEOs pursue a branding campaign when it is positioning that is required. Making matters worse, many folks don't know the difference between the two. Many think the two are synonymous. They aren't.
>
> Brand is ubiquity, where everyone knows you. Position is value, where everyone wants you. Brand's primary intent is to generate an emotional response from the intended audience where logical and legitimate product comparisons are difficult. Commodity-type products from multiple vendors with minimal differentiation are generally best served via branding, especially when price is the prime-determining factor or, as studies have shown, it is not a serious purchase that requires an extension of the self. Pick up a branded soap bar and move on.
>
> Brand provides recognition and awareness. Position helps the customer

Branding tells the story of your company. It's the perception of your company in the minds of your customers, employees and suppliers.

13

recite its attributes. It also takes time and time is money. Positioning can be done in a much shorter time frame (months not years) and is much less expensive and time-consuming.

For many industries and companies, especially where constant innovation is the vanguard of the market and market windows can be measured in six months or less, positioning is the best strategy for improving sales and market share, not branding. Besides, branding is difficult to measure and does not always show up in the form of sales.

This insistence on pursuing brand without articulating a position, or value position, contributed to the meltdown of many of the dotcoms. Companies embarked on brand identity campaigns, highlighted by 30-second commercials during the Super Bowl, thinking that if they could just get people to the web site, they would buy something. But there was no value proposition to get them to the site in the first place. Just because something can be done over the Internet does not mean there is value in doing so. And what is proving even more prescient, advertising during mega events works best for those already with a brand identity.

In high technology, there are companies that can claim to have true brand. Intel, Cisco, and Microsoft immediately come to mind. Sun Microsystems's brand is eroding and in serious need of a reposition and, until done so, and done so correctly and credibly, the company will continue to suffer.

In all cases, brand for these companies is defined by a position. Intel is the undisputed leader in microprocessors. Cisco makes networking equipment used in the development of the Internet. And try and find someone who doesn't do Windows. These companies do have brand in their respective markets. More importantly, their position is well recognized and understood.

Intel has tried to diversify into other markets, like all good companies should. But their $10 billion in venture investments into networking and communications infrastructure has yielded nada, according to their own CFO. They learned that the brand does not translate and nobody wants to be "Delled."

Hewlett-Packard is trying to repackage themselves as a consumer electronics company, announcing literally hundreds of products, few of which they actually intend to make themselves. But their underpinnings, their very credibility and brand identity have been their roots as a solid, dependable company with a deep understanding of technology. Carly Fiorina wants to shake up the company from its stodgy perceptions, leveraging the success and leadership in their printer division into a repositioning of the company as a consumer electronics powerhouse. Are you buying it?

Dell lost the Computer from its name and will probably follow HP into digital TVs and you can expect one if not both to be offering cell phones by the end of the year. There were almost 500 million cell phones sold last year and two, Motorola and Nokia, control more than half the market. Now tell me again why we need another cell phone company.

Gateway is transitioning from a computer company into a consumer electronics company, including a foray into retail outlets, and is one of the leading branded digital TV vendors. But the company is still not making money.

Yahoo has defied the tried-and-true test of brand building by developing a brand reputation very early. At the beginning of its young life, it could claim as its position to be all things Internet. This worked at the time, 1995 and 1996, as the Internet and the World Wide Web were still embryonic stages and people were looking for a company, or anybody, who could put definition to this new communications technology.

Because the stakes are so high and the competition so formidable, many smaller, emerging companies assign themselves the Herculean task of creating and implementing a branding campaign, when in reality, they should be picking the underserviced segments that their large competitive brethren are ignoring and attacking with an unassailable position and value proposition. Customers in these niche and very vertical markets are looking for a complete solution vs. a best-of-breed approach. They are not as tied to a single brand as the brand owners might think. If serviced properly, customers are more than willing to serve as reference accounts who can be leveraged as proof of concept. This reinforces their position as they tackle and transition into new market segments.

So don't worry about being all things to all people. The essence of positioning is that to be inclusive is to be exclusive. The key to a successful marketing campaign is to demonstrate value. This is best done through positioning, and is equally true in good economic times and bad.

Positioning is dynamic and fluid. Yesterday's unique position is today's commodity provider. Useful positioning describes who the company is, what it wants to be when it grows up, and why anyone should care.

Branding requires a continuous bombardment of a single message repeated ad nauseam. Effective positioning makes the customer a part of the unpaid sales team. Positioning leads to brand but brand does not always lead to position. Positioning is expected to change with the dynamics of marketplace. The essence of a brand is to provide rock-solid stability. Brand and position may live in the same house, but they are not necessarily related.

More importantly, positioning leads to sales. In today's volatile, though recovering, economic climate, who cares about anything else? In other words, why brand when positioning will do?

Slogans and Jingles

When you can identify radio and television commercials from the first few seconds of music, a particular voice, or the delivery of the first few lines, those companies are doing a great job of branding through advertising—especially if the ads evoke positive feelings. Jingles and slogans have been used to create and maintain branding identities for as long as most of us can remember.

We oldsters can still hum the Doublemint jingle or sing about cookies baked by little elves in a hollow tree. And we know which cereal is not for rabbits!

Using a slogan or jingle is a strong way to familiarize the public with your brand. Since it's unlikely that you have a budget to match those companies, it will take you longer to imprint your jingle or slogan ("Just do it," "Stronger than dirt," The Uncola") on your audience. Still, if you come up with something clever, people will remember. A slogan is free. A jingle is not.

If you're interested in having a jingle made, ask your radio rep(s) for a list of local and national outfits to talk with. You can have one done from a selection of pre-recorded jingles; your business name is plopped in and the jingle is yours to use within your own market, but not anywhere else. These jingles are less expensive, because they will be sold to other businesses like yours for use in other select markets. These are great for businesses with just one location or with several locations in different markets, because you can purchase the rights just for the specific areas you need. Slogans, on the other hand, need only brain cells—not money—to create.

People won't get sick of a good slogan or a good jingle. Lots of business owners tell me they don't want to advertise "too much" because they think people will overdose on their message. Huge companies advertise constantly, spending millions and millions of dollars, and they don't worry about people becoming bored. Familiarity is good!

Huge companies advertise constantly, spending millions and millions of dollars, and they don't worry about people becoming bored.

A small business budget, just because of its size, guarantees that you won't become boring. Most small businesses owners are thinking in terms of the expenditure itself, which seems huge, when in fact it's a very small amount of money compared with the millions spent by larger companies.

Jeffrey Detrick, Principal and Creative Director of Epicenter Advertising in San Diego, California (*www.epicenteradvertising.com*), sums up branding for us with his take on brand identity and managing your identity asset:

Your corporate and brand identities are among your most valuable strategic assets and must be planned and managed with great diligence to ensure their effectiveness.

Brand identity planning is not just a design issue—it is a strategic issue. Your corporate identity is a statement of how you view yourself as an organization and how you want to be viewed by others. In essence, it is a promise to all those who come in contact with you as to what they can expect from your company, from the professionalism of your people and the quality of your products, to the level of your customer service.

To be successful for the long term, your identity must clearly and consistently reflect the core messages that make your company unique. A strong corporate identity can have a profound impact on motivating audiences to choose your products or services for reasons beyond price and convenience, while also promoting an internal culture geared to sustaining customer relationships.

Ineffective identity management leads to a devaluation of the brand. If an identity is not consistent, it will fail, resulting in a fragmented set of names and identities, which do not communicate the organization's full scope.

A strategically focused identity system provides competitive advantages. It enables your organization to more effectively communicate who you are, what you do, and what makes you unique. The result? A better understanding of your organization, increased public recognition, and greater responsiveness to marketing messages.

These are the benefits of having a strong corporate identity:

▶ It enhances image and increases awareness.
▶ It builds a valuable asset for branding.
▶ It ensures a greater impact in marketing and advertising.
▶ It allows efficiencies through economies of scale.
▶ It provides winning recognition for accomplishments.
▶ It fosters a 'one team' corporate culture.
▶ It supports competitive differentiation.

The most important aspect of branding a product or service is to focus on defining, in very specific terms, the differentiating points of your product(s) or service(s) and those of your competitor(s), and then marketing those differentiators.

Rob Frankel (*www.robfrankel.com*), consultant and author of *The Revenge of Brand X: How to Build a Big Time Brand on the Web or Anywhere Else*, says:

> Branding is not about getting your prospects to choose you over your competition; it's about getting your prospects to see you as the only solution to their problem. In other words, in order to be chosen by the prospects, they have to feel like they can only get what they need from you. It makes you the only solution.
>
> Importantly, the more reasons you give them, the less important price becomes as a purchasing criterion. Which means the stronger your brand, the less important price becomes.

Check your own preferences for brands. How many of the following questions can you answer?

▶ What's your favorite brand of underwear?

▶ Which brand of orange juice do you buy?

▶ Which fabric softener do you use?

▶ What is your favorite brand of jeans?

▶ How many brands of peanut butter do you buy?

▶ Do you have a favorite kind of toothpaste?

▶ Which soap do you buy for the shower?

▶ Do you have a favorite florist?

▶ If you were ill, which hospital would you prefer?

▶ If you could watch only one news program on TV, which would it be?

▶ Which college would you like your child to attend?

TIP: Keep testimonials: If you are reliable and your product or service is liked and well priced, you will inevitably receive letters of thanks and even praise. Keep them in a binder and have them available and ready to show prospective customers who may be teetering on the edge of making a purchasing decision.

Your life is full of brands that you prefer over others. And chances are you can list the reasons why for each one of them right off the top of your head. For products, you even know which store carries them and on what shelf in what aisle they can be found. For the hospitals, schools, and television programs, you know where they are and why you favor them over the others that are available.

You want your customers to be able to list the reasons they come to you for a product or service as well. So, decide how you want your customers and potential customers to regard your business and then figure out how to get there.

Chapter 3

Public Relations

S ALLY SAVILLE HODGE, PRESIDENT OF HODGE COMMUNICATIONS, INC. IN Chicago, Illinois (*www.hodgecommunications.com*), says:

Many of the most successful businesses have established phenomenal growth without breaking their budgets on huge ad campaigns. Starbucks is one. Peapod, the online grocery delivery service, is another. What these companies have done is build awareness by creating a buzz about their products or services in a way that has produced a groundswell of interest, a growing, loyal customer base, and burgeoning sales.

Buzz marketing is really nothing more than word-of-mouth or the transfer of information through social networks. It has been around as long as people have been sharing ideas. But it's the smart business that has figured out ways to leverage the way word-of-mouth spreads on its own as a result of doing good business, to turn that natural occurrence into an important and powerful promotional tool. It doesn't take a huge budget to put a buzz marketing program in place. It doesn't require a trendy—or would-be trendy—product. It does, however, require that you understand your marketplace, because you must be able to tap into the power of influencers within it.

The art of buzz marketing has been gaining a whole new luster for various reasons in recent years. For one, the number of channels by which customers can be reached has been growing rapidly. The barrage of messages hits them on every front: television commercials, and infomercials that come off like television shows, radio spots, direct mail, internet sites, newsletters and e-newsletters, in movie trailers and movies themselves, point-of-purchase displays …. Well, you get the picture. Coming up with a compelling message that is able to break through all the clutter is increasingly problematic, particularly when too many businesses haven't come up with a way to solidly differentiate themselves from competitors and message around that difference.

Moreover, the public is increasingly skeptical in the face of all this noise confronting them. What it generally lacks is what customers are looking for—credibility. And if this is true of adults, it's a key trait of the hotly pursued Gen Y marketplace of children and young adults between ages 8 and 27, which places far more value on product recommendations made by their peers and people they admire than all the advertising in the world.

Bottom line … it can be cheap. And for businesses with limited budgets that need to get the word out, that's a pretty powerful argument for seeing if it will work for you. To understand how it works, consider some examples of businesses of varying sizes that have launched buzz campaigns.

Ford Motor Company: The target market for Ford's Focus model, introduced in 2000, was young adults. But rather than attempt to sway would-be buyers of this $13,000 subcompact version of its Escort model with a traditional advertising blitz, Ford opted for a buzz campaign aimed at influencers who want to stay on the cutting edge of cool. Its approach was to identify 120 influential young consumers in five major markets, who were each given the keys to a Focus and told to drive it for six months, keeping a record of where they went and what they did. As *Business Week* (July 30, 2001) recounted the results, the word spread virally through converts who became enthusiasts and, essentially, unpaid salespeople. One young man in Miami, for example, spotted a Focus in the parking lot of a leading hip-hop radio station, on loan for the duration to one of its hottest deejays. He was so taken that he pulled over, checked it out carefully, and even took photos. While waiting for his order of a special version of the car, he convinced his girlfriend to buy a Focus herself instead of the Civic (its top competitor) she had planned on. This kind of buzz helped put the Focus model on the map; it sold a whopping 286,166 units in its first full year.

Hebrew National: If buzz can boost sales of big-ticket items like automobiles, can it work on something as prosaic as hot dogs? The Hebrew National unit of ConAgra Foods believed so, and its experience proved that buzz marketing works for more than just the outrageous. The company recruited 250 PTA presidents, Hispanic community leaders, and even Jewish mothers from 12 major cities to serve on its "mom squad" several summers ago. Equipped with SUVs prominently displaying the Hebrew National logo, this ad hoc sales team descended on communities across the country, hosting backyard hot dog barbecues, distributing coupons at events, and cooking up sales that qualified the initiative as a success.

Buzz marketing is not risk-free. Because of its nature, you can't control it like you can with paid messaging. That means you have to plan and anticipate all the angles and possibilities for negative backlash. If you're trying to be subversive with your campaign and you're found out, you could cause more harm than good to your brand. IBM, for example, created a negative buzz several years ago when one of its agencies came up with a stealth campaign to leave wordless images of a peace symbol, a heart, and a penguin on Chicago and San Francisco sidewalks. The buzz was more about the way IBM ran afoul of the law for defacing public property than for its "Peace Love Linux" campaign behind open source software. More recently, buzz became shock when rock diva Janet Jackson "accidentally" bared her breast live during the 2004 Super Bowl festivities. Instead of bolstering a flagging career, the ill-advised move cost her the lead role in a pending movie profiling jazz great Lena Horne's life.

The buzz strategy is not risk-free, nor is it for every type of product. It's more difficult to employ it for something as mundane as, say, laundry detergent—where the odds of developing the kind of cult following normally associated with such a campaign are long, at best. Of course, that doesn't keep the big names from trying it out anyway. Procter & Gamble, for example, has employed buzz tactics to try to breathe new life into some of its older brands. One such effort in Canada had "shoppers," garbed in brightly colored duds, engage in impromptu fashion shows in supermarkets. Even though the brand, Cheer, wasn't sold hard, the so-called shoppers did mention that their outfits had been washed with the detergent. No word on how successful this campaign was.

Is a buzz marketing campaign a strategy that will help you grow your business? Consider some of the successes as well as the failures cited here. Then give serious thought to the kind of product you have and whether it has the kinds of buyers who might be well-disposed to the kind of positive word of mouth you're working at creating.

William J. McLaughlin, President of McLaughlin & Morgan, Inc. in Philadelphia, Pennsylvania (*www.mclaughlin-morgan.com*), offers the following advice:

> For small companies or new firms the best strategy is to go for the free press. Use PR out the wazoo (this is a technical advertising term). You don't have to be a PR pro to get some coverage. Pick up the phone and call the press. You may have to call more than once, or more than one person, but persistence will pay off.
>
> Know what you're going to say when you reach someone. If you have a web site, and every company should, you want to drive potential customers to it because it will be the epicenter of all business someday soon. So think content for it, and get the press to refer to it—it will bring you business.

Let your local media know that you are willing to be interviewed as a reliable expert when something newsworthy comes along.

Let your local media know that you are willing to be interviewed as a reliable expert when something newsworthy comes along. Send a note to the news departments of your local newspapers and radio and television stations, with a brief bio of yourself and topics you would be willing to comment on, should they need to contact an expert for a story. Being called upon in this way identifies you as a part of the community who can be trusted for an opinion or to provide accurate facts. Even if they want your take on a somewhat negative story, you still get credit for being an expert in your field. Michael Guzofsky, Creative Director of Pageworks Communication Design, Inc. in Denver, Colorado (*www.pageworksthebigidea.com*), tells us, "There's no such thing as bad publicity. Unless someone dies."

Another good piece of advice comes from Rosemary Brisco, President of ToTheWeb (*www.totheweb.com*) of San Mateo, California:

> Take advantage of free promotional opportunities and low-cost search engine ad buys. Trade publications and online portals are interested in free content. Write two or three short, information-packed articles that reflect your expertise and offer these without charge.

Robert Smith, President of Robert Smith & Associates PR in Rockton, IL, (*www.robertsmith.citymax.com*) provides an alternate method to a standard news release—the pitch letter.

> If an editor receives a pitch letter that speaks to an article she is planning, she may contact you for an interview. Sending pitch letters is highly effective because editors, program directors, and reporters are constantly on the lookout for accessible expert sources they can call to get a quote.
>
> So, how do you find out stories that reporters are working on? There are two ways. The first is to contact reporters at publications that interest you and ask them what they are working on. The second way is to contact the advertising

department of a publication and request a media kit. Included in this kit is an editorial calendar that lists different topics/subjects or stories for the entire year.

Once you know stories that a reporter is working on, … you send your pitch letter. This is an excellent strategy to get into publications that normally wouldn't talk to you. If, for example, a large business magazine is working on a story on fast-growing minority companies, your pitch letter should look like this:

> Dear Sam Jones:
>
> In your coverage of fast-rising minority-owned companies in Illinois, I'd like to offer my expertise to help enhance your article.
>
> Minority-owned businesses have high failure rates and I'm glad to hear that you are taking the time to highlight a few success stories.
>
> It's important to your readers that our society as a whole is represented and I applaud your publication for doing that. As a 30-year-old, African-American entrepreneur, I've made it through obstacles and adversity to build one of the biggest PR firms in northern Illinois.
>
> My revenues have grown 234 percent since 2001, and it's been because of joint ventures and partnerships with other companies.
>
> If you would like to arrange an interview, please contact me at 815-555-1497.
>
> Sincerely,
>
> John Doe

Public relations goes hand in hand with advertising. It won't take the place of advertising, but can enhance it tremendously. Remember how Mrs. Fields handed out her chocolate chip cookies to people outside of her store when she first started? Personal contact is a great form of PR.

I remember going to a baby shower and seeing a cake made to look like a carriage. The woman who baked the cake owned a bakery and was a guest at the shower. She took home three orders and every other guest asked for her card!

A neighbor of mine owns a glass shop and brings a bottle of glass cleaner to every party he attends. He gets lots of orders that way and the other guests are always intrigued at the odd hostess gift and ask about it, so he gets new customers that way too.

A few yeas ago I designed brochures for a diet business. The brochure featured a pudgy cartoon police officer with the heading "Turn Yourself In." It offered a special deal for police officers. We distributed the brochures to city and county police stations with great results.

Opportunities to show your stuff are everywhere. Just look for them!

Public relations goes hand in hand with advertising. It won't take the place of advertising, but can enhance it tremendously.

23

Chapter 4

Maintain Your Customer Base

WHILE YOU'RE IN THE PROCESS OF ADVERTISING, REMEMBER not to overlook your valuable existing customers while you work to intrigue new ones. The point is to hang on to the current base while encouraging more to join. If you're building a brick wall, and every time you add a new brick you find that someone has removed the last brick you added, you're going nowhere fast. (Picture a hamster in one of those little wheels.) Each brick you lose slows the building process. And trust me when I say that there are other business owners who will be constantly trying to take your bricks as fast as you can put them into your wall.

There are ways to "tie up" customers right from their first purchase—ways to keep them with you for at least one more contact.

- ▶ Retailers can stuff each bag that leaves their store with a coupon good for a percentage off the next purchase. (Put an end date on it.)

- ▶ House painters can get first contracts by offering a free trim touchup two years down the road. That contact may be enough for the customer to call that painter back in another two years when the whole house needs to be done again. The painter can provide an original color paint chip that the owner can match to the house to show how faded it's getting over time.

▶ Landscapers can offer a free or a reduced-cost fertilizing session every spring to those who sign up for mowing, planting, or snow removal. A pack of seeds or bulbs delivered each spring will remind customers that you're interested in maintaining their business.

▶ Florists can provide a valuable reminder service to customers. Ask clients to fill out cards with anniversary dates, birthdays, etc. and offer to call and remind them a week ahead of time.

▶ Beauty shops can provide a complimentary bottle of shampoo or conditioner (perhaps a new product that you're carrying) after every ten hair appointments or just a free bottle of nail polish (the client's favorite shade) after ten manicures.

▶ Pet stores can set aside a day to take a photo of customers with their pets—with or without Santa or the Easter Bunny! Or purchase small sample bags of a new brand of snacks for dogs or cats or birds, etc. and give one out with each appropriate purchase. Make your customers happy and they'll come back!

Each happy customer is a vote of confidence for your business and the opportunity for you to receive word-of-mouth praise to others. Take care of your customers, new and old, and they'll take care of you.

Expansion

I went to a local pet shop last month to buy food for my parakeet. The store had started to carry puppies and I couldn't get myself out of the store without oohing and aahing over the tiny balls of fur running in a spacious open pen (so the rest of the saps and I could pet them). When I walked two stores down to the office supply store, I gushed to the cashier about the puppies— how I had never seen a baby greyhound and that it looked like a tiny little deer and how the black spaniel's eyes begged for the attention I was more than happy to provide. I am sure that at least two other people in line heard me blathering about the different puppies and my guess is that at least one of them went to take a peek. I may not be in the market for a dog, but I know that I will naturally be telling more people about those pups because it was such a fun experience for me. And I won't go to the other pet store in town now to buy my bird food, because they don't carry puppies and I will want to repeat the experience.

Note: Before long later I returned to purchase more bird food. One of the puppies bit me and tore a hole in the arm of my new sweater. So much for the joyful experience of petting the furballs, and now I don't care where I buy my bird food. Perhaps a "please don't pet the puppies" sign would have been a good idea. It might have saved the store a customer!

Look for ways to maintain your businesses by offering better prices for longer-term contracts or expanding your residential business to include commercial. This is a natural way for painters, decorators, lawn care specialists, cleaning services, florists, driveway installation, etc., to pick up commercial business that pays more and deals in long-term contracts. Retailers should provide their customers with discount coupons for their next few purchases to encourage them to return. It is possible to encourage coupon redemption, and even set the pace of redemption, by making each coupon valid for different weeks or months. Tom Matzell, President and Creative Director of MRW Communications (*www.mrwinc.com*) in Boston, says,

Look for ways to maintain your businesses by offering better prices for longer-term contracts or expanding your residential business to include commercial.

> Value-added service is king in today's marketplace. Do a good job at that and word-of-mouth advertising will bring you more customers than any other medium you could pay for.

You have a responsibility to yourself and the enterprise you have undertaken to constantly think of new and creative ways to increase your business. If your company lends itself to sharing advertising with someone else, don't be afraid to approach another business owner.

Karen Krizman, President of MCM Communications in Harrison, New York, says,

> Another way to increase revenue and retain the customer base is to add complementary products or services to a business's already existing product/service mix. This provides ease and convenience to the customers, giving them a "one-stop shopping" experience.

> **Example:** A woman whose small business offered health and fitness training began struggling when the economy turned downward. It was difficult to justify the expense of trying to acquire new clients when most clients were cutting back or doing without. However, she realized that existing customers were already aligned to this type of service, so she began offering nutrition counseling, along with meditation. She increased her revenue from existing clients and the additional services attracted new clients.

Strategic Alliances/Partnerships

Krizman offers the following suggestions:

> There are several strategies available to maintain, or even increase, revenue

by exploring non-traditional partnerships and revenue streams, including strategic alliances and partnerships.

One way to add revenue is for a business to align itself with another company whose product or service complements its own, but does not directly compete. Another way is to partner with a company whose target market is similar, yet offers very different products or services.

Example: An education publisher wanted to increase revenue generated from its catalog. Instead of investing in new products or increasing prices, this company approached other education publishers and supplemental materials suppliers, offering the opportunity to promote their products through the catalog. These companies could now reach almost one million educators for free. In exchange, our publisher would realize 40 percent of the proceeds from the sale of the partners' products.

However, don't get into shared advertising opportunities with businesses you don't know.

▶ If they end up not paying, you will get stuck paying their half of the media bills just to keep your own credit in good standing. It is best to have both parties put the money in upfront to avoid the possibility of one or the other business paying its half late or not at all.

▶ If your advertising partner doesn't come through with promises it makes regarding products or services, unhappy customers will link your two businesses in their minds forever. On the other hand, hooking up with an established business with a good reputation is a wonderful opportunity to add credibility to your own company name.

Don't be afraid of rejection. You will find that many small companies are eager to hear about creative, cooperative plans to promote their business. You can make projects like this happen for your business.

List some businesses that might be interested in sharing a promotional project with you:

1.

2.

3.

4.

5.

Sponsorships

Sponsorships are another way to maintain and build your business, Krizman suggests:

> A third method to increase or maintain revenue is to approach large companies who share the same demographic target audience to sponsor a special event or offering. The key here is to be able to offer significant exposure for the larger company so they may justify the expense.

> **Example:** Our small education publisher developed a value-added online field trip for their subscribers. Kid correspondents from around the country would attend major events (e.g., the Super Bowl), interview key figures, and report online. The publisher obtained sponsorship from a very large athletic apparel company who sells to teens and tweens. The apparel company's contribution offset all travel, lodging, database, and other associated costs, while providing a small profit to the publisher.

Seminars

Mark Levit, Managing Partner of Partners and Levit, Inc. in New York, New York (*www.partnerslevit.com*), says:

Smart marketers have recognized the seminar as one of the most cost-effective ways to sell their products and services.

> Imagine a room full of sales prospects focusing on you and your every word. Imagine each one taking notes, asking questions, and recognizing you as one of the foremost authorities in your industry.

> Do you think you could grow your business with that level of respect and authority? You bet you could! It's done every day by insurance executives, web developers, bankers, food manufacturers, real estate professionals, software developers, and others.

> Smart marketers have recognized the seminar at one of the most cost-effective ways to sell their products and services. It is an effective medium to address many prospects as a single venue. The lure for the prospect is business education on a topic of interest to them. Their payment to you, the seminar sponsor, is to endure a short commercial about your product or service. Seminars advance prospects along the sales continuum by establishing a relationship with the marketer. Seminars turn a faceless vendor into a familiar expert.

> To be effective, seminars should have a strong educational element wherein attendees learn new facets of a topic of current interest. They must be soft on the "sell." A brief description of what you offer will enable you to

follow up after the event. In most categories, sales cannot be consummated until trust is earned. A soft sell signals you're not just interested in your prospects' money; you are there to provide "value added" to establish trust.

The speaker featured at your seminar can be a widely known expert, author, government official, or journalist. Properly promoted, prospects will attend to learn from the expert. After the featured presentation, the speaker "passes off" his or her credibility to a company spokesperson that makes a brief presentation on the sponsoring company's offerings.

My company has often arranged for the media to co-sponsor such events for its clients—especially when the client is a frequent advertiser in a publication or broadcast outlet. That kind of co-branding adds credibility to the seminar sponsor's offer. And often, the media will foot part of the bill!

Ironically, even though admission is offered on a complimentary basis, a lot of effort goes into generating adequate attendance. Invitations must go out early, follow-up telephone calls must be made to encourage attendance—and reminder telephone calls have to be made the day before the seminar to remind well-intentioned guests to attend. Remember that your prospects are busy!

Breakfast or luncheon seminars are recommended when conducting seminars for senior managers who generally won't attend after work.

You can also hold paid seminars and charge a fee to people who are interested in learning what you know. Be sure to provide a healthy dose of valuable information and materials so those who attended will feel that they received a great deal for the money they spent, so that you will be able to do it again in the future!

You can handle the whole seminar by yourself or gather a few experts together and divide up the time between speakers. Be sure and allow a Q&A session at the end and if you have a book, CD, or other such materials available for sale, let that be known at that time or include the price of a copy in your registration price.

Once you know the total cost of the space you're renting, food you may be providing, audio/visual equipment or any other costs you incur, and the amount you will charge each person to attend, you can calculate the minimum number of people who must register.

Let those who register know that you need a certain amount of people to register in order to hold the seminar and ask that registration and payment be sent to you by a specific date. The date is usually the last day by which you can cancel your rental space or ads without incurring a penalty.

If you have to cancel, return the payments you received promptly with an apology and perhaps a coupon good for 10 percent off the next seminar of yours that they register for.

Figure 4-1 shows an ad I used for a seminar.

Figure 4-2 shows a sample seminar budget worksheet provided by Levit.

Advertising Seminar for New and Small Businesses

You have to advertise, but don't waste your money in the process.

Tuesday, February 19, 2002

Holiday Inn (7th North & Electronics Pkwy) 9am – 2pm

Kathy Kobliski, author, columnist, and owner of Silent Partner Advertising, helps you understand the necessity of advertising your business, simplifies the process, and provides you with the tools to advertise on a small budget. Learn about building your brand, how to take control of your budget, and where to find help. $70.00 includes 4-hour seminar, a copy of *Advertising Without an Agency*, and lunch. A minimum of 15 people must register. Call 487-6706 or send completed form to: Silent Partner Advertising, 106 Peridot Drive, Syracuse, NY 13219.

Name _____

Company _____

Mailing address _____

Daytime phone _____

E-mail _____

Mail completed form with check for $70.00 by February 11, 2002, to: Silent Partner Advertising, 106 Peridot Drive, Syracuse, NY 13219

Figure 4-1. Example of copy for a seminar ad

Seminar Budget Worksheet

Event	Food and Beverages	Incidentals
_____ _____	Caterer's Menu _____ Wine/Liquor _____ Mixers _____ Ice _____ Other _____ **Subtotal** _____	Pads _____ Pens _____ Name Badges _____ Place Cards _____ Gifts/Giveaways _____ Gift Bags _____ **Subtotal** _____
Date/Time	**Invitations**	**Miscellaneous**
_____ _____ **Purpose** _____ _____	Design _____ Printing Charges _____ Addressing _____ Postage _____ **Subtotal** _____	Total Sales Tax _____ Service Charges _____ Tips _____ Other _____ **Subtotal** _____
Number of Guests	**Equipment Rentals**	**Totals**
_____ _____ **Proposed Budget** _____ _____	Tables _____ Chairs _____ Projector _____ Laptop Computer _____ Internet Connection _____ Miscellaneous _____ Other _____ **Subtotal** _____	Combined Subtotals _____ Contingency Allowance (Approx 10%) _____ **Total Expenses** _____
Event Space	**Presentation**	**Notes**
Rental Fee for Space _____ Insurance _____ Other _____ **Subtotal** _____	Keynote Speaker _____ Guest Speaker _____ Posters _____ Signage _____ Products or Literature _____ Other _____ **Subtotal** _____	_____ _____ _____ _____ _____ _____ _____

Figure 4-2. Seminar budget worksheet (continued on the next page)

Seminar Budget Worksheet		
Transportation		**Notes**
Chartered Buses _____		_____
Limousines _____		_____
Hostesses		_____
(if needed) _____		_____
Other _____		_____
Subtotal _____		_____
		_____
		_____
Staff	**Publicity**	**Notes**
Meeting Planner ____	Publicist _____	_____
Waitstaff _____	Press Releases _____	_____
Cleanup Help _____	Press Kit _____	_____
Coat-Check	Printing _____	_____
Attendants _____	Postage _____	_____
Parking	Photographer _____	_____
Attendants _____	Other _____	_____
Security Guards ____	**Subtotal** _____	_____
Other _____		_____
Subtotal _____		

Figure 4-2. Seminar budget worksheet (continued)

Keep in Touch: Don't Take Your Customers for Granted

Apathy is one the largest reasons for the loss of a customer, especially if you are in a service industry. After you work with someone for a substantial amount of time, you may start to let the account or the person slide, feeling that you have that one in the bag. But once customers or clients start to feel that you are taking them for granted, that they may not be receiving the same amount of attention or care that they used to, they are ripe for the picking by a new service person. Make calls to see how things are going and ask if there's anything they need from you now and then. Time slips by and you may not realize how long it has been since you've made a courtesy call. Don't get comfortable. Do it now!

Say Thank You!

It's a simple way to maintain your customer base, but it's often overlooked. Show your customers that you appreciate their loyalty with a special offer, a little gift, or even an open house with holiday refreshments at your location. As a retailer, you must be dollar-wise when choosing a way to say thank you if you have hundreds of customers. In this case, a special offer through the mail or on your web site is a good idea. For businesses that deal with fewer, but large clients, a gift is more in order. Gift certificates for a dinner at a special restaurant, a holiday wreath or ornament if that's appropriate, assortments of cookies or other goodies—all say thank you in a way that will be remembered. Job-related items work too. For example, a contractor I know received a large, engraved level from a store he frequented for building supplies. The engraving on this level, which was about three feet long, said, "Thank you for your business." Actually, even I was impressed and all I know about tools is what I've learned from walking by the ones hung in our garage. But I could tell just from looking that this was an expensive level and that it was a smart thank-you gift to this builder. Every time he picked the thing up he would remember who had given it to him. You may opt to do something big once a year or a few smaller things throughout the year. Either way, it always pays to let your customers know they're important to you.

Show your customers that you appreciate their loyalty with a special offer, a little gift, or even an open house with holiday refreshments at your location.

33

Chapter 5

Define Your Market

N
O MATTER HOW LARGE OR SMALL YOUR ADVERTISING BUDGET IS, no matter what obstacles you face, you have got to do the basics ... and do them well. That means you have to understand your market, your product/service category, your competition, your potential target audiences, claims you can make that haven't been "taken," and what your product provides that fills a real need. Put it on one page. Write it on the back of an envelope. But do your homework before you start spending a penny of your budget on advertising. If you want to swim with the sharks, you better think the same way they do!

You may think you know what segment of the population makes up your customer base—male, female, or both genders, young, middle-aged, or older. Hopefully, before you decided to open your business you had experience working in a similar business and have at least some grasp of who your customers should be.

The segments of a demographic group are *age* and *gender*. In the gender category, you choose between *female* and *male* or, if your customers are fairly evenly divided, *adults*. Age ranges are 18-34, 18-49, 25-54, and 45+. Those are the two determinations you make.

The group of 18-34 seems like it could be synonymous with 18-49. But 18-34 represents the younger segment of the two groups, ending a full 15 years short of the larger group. Therefore, a business catering to teens or people in their 20s would choose to advertise to the 18-34 group rather than choosing 18-49, simply because it doesn't want to waste money reaching people too old for its product.

The 18-49 group fits within the 25-54 range. But you will reach the younger portion of that population segment (ending around age 35) by using 18-49 and reach the older people in that group (35-54) in the 25-54 group.

The same goes for the 25-54 segment and the 45+ group. The 45+ group represents persons age 45 and up—baby boomers—including seasoned citizens, grandparents, and retired people. While you may reach some of these people using 25-54, you would mainly be reaching people too young for your product or service. Your major target group is 45+.

At one time 18-34 was rarely used; it was included in the wider range of 18-49. However, there is a huge difference, for example, in musical tastes of an 18-year-old and a 49-year-old—the opposite ends of that 18-49 spectrum—so the 18-34 group was created to break down the larger segment. It allows us to see where the younger portion of that group tunes in and where the older portion settles in to listen. The same principle applies to the overlapping of the other age groups.

In order to decide where to best place your advertising dollars, it is necessary to first break your customer base into primary and secondary demographic groups. You will use the lion's share of your budget to reach your primary group—and if your budget is very small, you will use it all on that group.

Tom Matzell, President and Creative Director of MRW Communications (*www.mrwinc.com*) in Boston, tells us:

In order to decide where to best place your advertising dollars, it is necessary to first break your customer base into primary and secondary demographic groups.

Too many advertisers (big and small) ignore or do not place enough emphasis on the first stage of any advertising campaign—identifying and understanding the target audience. Without this knowledge, any campaign is doomed to failure. Small businesses especially need to take the time to find out exactly who their potential customers are, how far they are willing to come to buy products, what they need, what they are looking for, what you can provide that others can't, etc. Know everything you can about your customer base. How? Use the internet to search for published materials on consumer behavior (there's a ton of it out there). Poll your own customer base by mail, on the net, or in the store. Analyze who is your competition and how they approach the same customer base. Until you know as much as you can about your customers, how can you effectively decide where and when to advertise and what to promote? Once you have a clear idea of who it is you need to talk to, the most cost-effective advertising choices on how to reach them will be apparent.

Let's take college students as an example of a specific target group. Most colleges and universities have their own newspapers and often their own campus radio stations with ad space for sale. That always seems like a good place to start when trying to reach this group of people.

But you also have to look beyond the fact that these adults are in college and approach them demographically (by age and gender). They make up a good portion of the 18- to 35-year-old population, so you can also reach them via appropriate non-student radio stations, TV shows, and publications, all of which have audiences made up of very specific demographic groups. It's age and gender that bind these audiences together, not individual traits, habits, and hobbies.

You still have to decide if you're looking for males, females, or both. Reaching a group as specific as "college students" is no less easy because they live in groups, do a lot of walking, carry books, write a lot of papers, and maybe drink a beer or two on the weekends, than it is to reach any other group of people. It's a no-brainer that they are prime candidates for casual shoes, computers and related software, and yes, even beer (sigh). You still have to decide if you can make their lives easier, studying more convenient, clothes and shoes more comfy, etc. and find the best way to let them know.

It all boils down to understanding more than one thing about the people you're trying to reach—in this case, more than the fact that college students go to college. Yes, that's important because you know their physical whereabouts for most of the year. But where do they eat their meals? What do they eat? Where do they shop? How do they get around? How do they pay for products? Do they bank locally or get money from home? What's the climate like where they live? Are they buying hot soup or iced coffee? Parkas or bathing suits? Tires for their mountain bikes or snow tires for their trucks? Sandals for the beach or insulated boots? Clearly, the fact that they all go to college can't be the only factor in deciding how to reach these people.

Mark Ramsey, President of Mercury Radio Research in San Diego, California (*www.mercradio.com*), says,

> One would hope that direct advertisers have a sense of what makes their audience qualitatively unique. That is, all men 25-34 are not alike. Upscale, downscale, family man, party animal—these distinctions are not part of the equation for the station reps—but to the clients, they're key.

When hunters wake up in the morning, they know what they're tracking that day and where they need to go to find their game. If they're hunting deer, they won't sit in a boat in flooded timber, because that's not where deer will be. If they're hunting ducks, they won't sit in a tree in the middle of a snow-covered forest, because they know they'll go home empty-handed.

Let's say our hunters have decided on ducks. That's a good start, but what kind of ducks? Mallards? Pintails? Wood ducks? Not all ducks are found in the same swamp—or even in the same state. Hunters have to know where to find specific kinds of ducks and go to their natural habitats.

You have to do the same thing. Be able to identify your specific customers and know exactly where to find them. Are you looking for women? Great—but you won't find an 18-year-old woman and a 45-year-old woman listening to the same music, watching the same television program, reading the same publications, or checking the same web sites. Know them like the hunters know their ducks and get specific!

Delivering your message to the right people, and doing it with enough frequency to give them a chance to hear and understand the message, is the whole story of advertising.

Delivering your message to the right people, and doing it with enough frequency to give them a chance to hear and understand the message, is the whole story of advertising. The first critical step of determining who the right people are is the one you are about to take. You may find after some thought that the answer might not be as obvious as you believed.

When you feel you have identified your primary customers, circle the correct choices from Groups A and B. You may need to circle more than one age choice from Group A. From Group B, you will circle only one option. Does your business lend itself primarily to males, females, or both? (If both, you will circle Adults.) You will now use this information to identify radio and television stations and publications targeting the groups you have selected. These choices are the basis for all of your media planning and media buying. This is the information from which all advertising decisions are made, so give careful thought to your selections.

Primary Market

Group A (Age)	Group B (Gender)
18-34	Male
18-49	Female
25-54	Adults
45+	

To simplify the demographic choices you need to make and compensate for the overlapping of ages, use the following guidelines until you develop a feel for the process:

- ▶ If you estimate your customers to be 12-24 years of age, circle the 18-34 group.
- ▶ If you estimate your customers to be 25-35 years of age, circle the 18-49 group.
- ▶ If you estimate your customers to be 36-50 years of age, circle the 25-54 group.
- ▶ If you estimate your customers to be over 50 years of age, circle the 45+ group.

A car dealer may circle all of the age choices in Group A, because everyone who can drive is a potential customer. Then again, he may consider one demographic group for his brand-new luxury models, another for the more economical models, and still another for used cars. Other types of businesses will have a very narrow selection for a primary choice and another very specific group circled for the secondary market.

The people who make up your secondary demographic group can be elusive—and putting a bull's-eye on them is more difficult.

How do you identify your secondary market? In some ways, this can be a bigger challenge than tagging your primary group. The people who make up your secondary demographic group can be elusive—and putting a bull's-eye on them is more difficult. For this group, you need to put some thought into who interacts with your primary demographic group the most.

For instance, I am a 58-year-old female. Businesses catering to 45+-year-old females—like cars, clothing, grocery stores, weight-loss clinics, vitamins, etc.—would know they could send their message to me on the stations and programs catering to the 45+ Female demographic group. Easy, right? Well ....

- ▶ I am also a wife and I buy 90% of my husband's clothes. His hobbies include hunting and railroad modeling, so I need to be informed on those topics.
- ▶ I have three sons:
  - The oldest is a 32-year-old corporate bond trader and the father of two. His hobby is also hunting. And forget shopping for my grandchildren: that can range from toys, to clothes, to CDs, to bedding.
  - Son #2 is a 30-year-old police officer who is interested in physical fitness. I shop for holiday and birthday gifts for him that include clothes, CDs, DVDs, lottery subscriptions, and concert tickets. He is getting married soon and that involves me in some of the wedding preparations: invitations to the rehearsal dinner and the rehearsal dinner itself, flowers, tuxedos, hotel accommodations for our out-of-town guests, and more.

– Son #3 is 20 years old. I shop for clothes, movie passes, computer games and programs, video games, college supplies, and a whole different set of products and services than I deal with for his father and older brothers.

Would you think of advertising to a 58-year-old woman for the following items?

▶ Video games, CDs, DVDs, computer software

▶ Toys and clothes for 6- and 7-year-old children

▶ Wedding products and services

▶ Hunting gear, including guns, ammunition, camouflage outerwear, etc.

While I may not be your primary audience, I surely am a strong secondary.

You must think very hard about the people you want to reach. Your conclusions will not only guide your decisions on where to consistently place your advertising dollars, but allow you to take advantage of affordable promotions or advertising packages proposed to you by reps of stations or programs you don't normally consider. Think hard, and then identify your secondary market.

Secondary Market

Group A (Age)	Group B (Gender)
18-34	Male
18-49	Female
25-54	Adults
45+	

A small budget doesn't allow much experimentation. Common sense dictates that you target your primary audience first, then the secondary group. Start by reaching your primary group closest to your location, and then work your way out geographically. Before you finish this book, you will read about various forms of advertising that let you be geographically specific as well as demographically specific—such as direct mail, some forms of print, outdoor advertising, and even cable TV.

Your customer base can change with the addition of new merchandise to your inventory or services you provide, a shift in the community caused by the opening or closing of a university, an industry, a military base, or just the natural aging of people in the community. It is a good idea to keep track of your customers—not only during your first weeks and months, but throughout your business life, so they don't move on and leave you behind!

Envision the daily life of your target consumers—every moment from the time they wake up to the time they go back to bed. Where would your product or service fit in? What problem would it solve? What benefit can you show that will make that person believe your product or service is not a desire, but a necessity? If it solves a financial problem, makes the neighbors jealous, provides a health-related improvement, gives a psychological or physical boost, gives an edge or an advantage over a competitor—whatever the benefit may be, show it, say it, make them believe it—and you've got a sale. Seek them out. Don't wait for them to find you.

The Customer Information Worksheet (shown filled in) will allow you to track changes in your customer base and provide facts you need to make proper advertising decisions. At least twice a year for a three- or four-week period, keep these worksheets by your register on a clipboard. Ask for each purchaser's ZIP code, fill in the gender section, and estimate the age. Analyzing this information will provide, along with the demographic facts for selecting radio and television stations, the ZIP code data you need to help you with direct mail and outdoor advertising. It will allow you to evaluate changes in your customer base and respond accordingly.

After each sheet is completed, total the columns and list in order the top five ZIP codes, the numbers of males and females, and the number of people falling into each age group at the bottom of the page. As you begin analyzing your Customer Information Worksheets, the results will either validate your original assessment of who your customers are or give you a clearer picture of them. If over time the numbers in the columns change, you will be ready to react—not only with your service or product lines, but also with your advertising decisions.

Your salespeople will, in all probability, resist this step. It's a good idea to hold a small meeting to go over these sheets to explain why it is important that they be used consistently. Tell your employees that the information will provide you with facts you need to advertise to the right people and that advertising to the right people is a huge part of what will make your business a success. Make them feel that they are doing something really important for themselves as well as for the business. After all, without a successful business, you have no jobs for them!

Now that you've defined your business and you've determined exactly what your ideal customer looks like, you're ready to meet the people who will want to become your new best friends—media sales reps!

CUSTOMER INFORMATION WORKSHEET		
Dates: From _____ to _____		
ZIP Codes	Gender	Age (estimate)
13219	F	26
13010	F	32
13689	F	20
13219	M	24
13219	F	31
13842	F	35
13209	F	27
13689	M	27
13010	F	30
13219	M	18
13219	F	21
13842	F	24
13219	F	19
13010	M	20
13842	F	21
13010	F	26
13219	M	32
13842	F	30
13010	F	26
13010	F	26
13219	M	32
13842	F	30
13010	F	26
TOTALS		
13219 (8)		12-24 (8)
13010 (7)	Females (17)	25-35 (15)
13842 (5)		36-50 (0)
13689 (2)	Males (6)	Over 50 (0)
13209 (1)		

Figure 5-1. Sample customer information worksheet

Chapter 6

Media Sales Reps

MEDIA SALES REPRESENTATIVES, AKA ACCOUNT EXECUTIVES, ARE among the friendliest, good-humored, and persuasive people you will meet in your career as a business owner. You will find it easy to become friends with many of them and easy to be flattered by the attention they give, the lunches and concert tickets they can provide. If all goes well, you will enjoy the time you spend with those who represent the stations and publications and other forms of media you need.

Your media account executives work within an ever-changing environment. Competition and change are the two constants in the world of media sales. Market forces, changes in station ratings, unacceptable sales performance, and many other factors can cause sales reps to move, voluntarily or otherwise, from one employer to another.

It can be difficult to see a favorite sales rep who has been calling on you from radio station A suddenly show up at your door as an energetic rep from radio station B and later yet as a sales rep from the daily newspaper. You can start to wonder about his or her objectivity and question any advertising advice you may have received from that rep in the past. It may be the first time you see this person as a sales representative whose goal it is to persuade you to do business with whatever station or publication he or she represents. As friendly and fun as they can be, media reps are working tirelessly to meet tough budgets and will try hard to dissuade you from placing your advertising dollars elsewhere. It is what they are trained to do.

Every sales staff is trained differently. The type of training can be directly linked to the size and financial condition of the company they work for.

For instance, radio and television stations with large audiences, high ratings, and therefore high rates are able to send their sales people to fairly lavish training sessions and hire expensive consultants to hone and perfect every sales skill. Stations with small audiences and lower operating budgets (since the two are hopelessly intertwined) cannot afford that level of extravagance and will rely on a sharp, experienced sales manager to work with each individual account executive as well as with the group as a whole to be creative and competent in the field.

Every sales staff is trained differently. The type of training can be directly linked to the size and financial condition of the company they work

Managers of both kinds of stations will put together promotion-oriented packages hoping to draw you in with the excitement of a big event. Both sales teams learn the art of cold calling, although smaller stations will do more of it by necessity.

Every radio and television salesperson quickly learns how to interpret the ratings of his or her station and how to put the best light on its current standing in the market. After each new "book" has arrived, it is the job of each rep to put the best spin on whatever Arbitron or Nielsen had to say. Trust me when I tell you that each station in the market can and will come up with a plausible case for you to cough up your advertising dollars. The case may be made *because* of the numbers and it may also be made *in spite* of the numbers. Mark Ramsey of Mercury Radio Research states:

The best way to protect yourself from being sold a bill of goods is to understand your market and press the station representatives to demonstrate that their audiences match your market. If they can't prove it, out the door they should go. Further, you should demand testimonials from your peers, either across the street or across the country. Every industry has a community of companies with the same problems, and the solutions of others might be yours as well. For example, ask, "Has WXXX worked for a company like yours? Where's the proof? Have sales increased as a result of running a healthy schedule or not?" The answer comes down to knowing your market and forcing the station reps to prove that their stations can deliver not just bodies, but results—and results for your product, your market.

You may find that dealing with your print, direct mail, and outdoor advertising account executives is a little more relaxed, although there will still be competition between daily and weekly papers and between competing dailies if you're lucky enough to have more than one in your area.

There will never be as large a number of competing direct mail and outdoor companies or publications in one market as there are competing radio and television stations. Although these reps are also calling on you with the intent of capturing your advertising dollars, they do not have as much individual competition to sell against once they have your interest. The most difficult part of their job is to sway you away from the glitz and glamour of radio and television in general and toward their particular *type* of media.

One of the first questions all reps will ask is "What budget are you working with?" Whether you believe it or not, they are not asking this to determine what their commission will be. A good rep knows that a very small budget with low frequency—be it print or electronic—will not produce the desired results and will be hesitant to run a schedule almost certainly doomed to failure. That scenario always ends up with a disappointed business owner and a rep who has little chance of a continuing relationship. The station or paper looks ineffective and will probably not be used again by the client.

Once you decide to work with any rep, from radio, television, print, outdoor, or direct mail, be sure to provide an accurate budget figure.

Once you decide to work with any rep, from radio, television, print, outdoor, or direct mail, be sure to provide an accurate budget figure so he or she can put together a realistic proposal for you—and don't hold back. If you can spend $8,000-$10,000 in one week, then say it! You wouldn't expect a real estate agent to find you a house without knowing what you can afford to spend. It's exactly the same with advertising. The possible combinations are too overwhelming to put down on paper without knowing what you can afford.

If you are planning to put together your media buy *after* you accept proposals from *all* of your reps, let that be known. Then they will know that they have to share the budget and each rep will work to give you the best deal possible to entice you to place a large share of your budget with him or her.

The professional media account executive understands every aspect of his or her business. The production people, on-air personalities, and art directors have their own areas of expertise, as do the people in traffic, news, and promotion departments. They take little or no interest in the sales department. But sales reps know *every* aspect of each of those areas as well as their own. Most of your reps are hard-working professionals who truly care that your advertising works for you. Not only will successful media campaigns mean repeat business for them, but they enjoy and take pride in helping your business to grow. They will be listening closely to whatever you tell them about your business, so be sure you provide the most accurate information possible.

Mike Dardano, Chief Facilitator at Adpotential in Mount Kisco, New York (*www.adpotential.com*), says:

> Today's consumer is being bombarded by hundreds of advertising and sales messages each day. The onslaught of these appeals to a stressed out and time-strapped audience is overwhelming. In addition, there is more media fragmentation than ever. Although the media is consolidating, the amount of different communication channels continues to grow each year with the addition of in-theater advertising, multi-media cell phones, and product placements in television. For all media the ability to stick out from all the clutter and win passionate eyeballs, readers, and listeners is more challenging than ever.

> In addition, clients are looking for a solid return on their investment. They want results from their advertising and marketing and will not tolerate image-only studies that claim to have raised awareness. With this new era of cost controls and communication clutter, it is imperative that media reps from TV and radio offer more than just a desirable time slot. They have to be media consultants and work with the client and agency on how their respective medium fits into the media mix. The media rep has to distinguish the value proposition of the offer and then discuss their media plan in totality. Only after a good picture of the client's goals, message, and target is understood can they come up with a solution that fits into these objectives.

> Knowing other media is not a strong suit of media reps. They usually only know about their medium or station and are clueless about other media in their marketplace. The media companies do not pay their reps to know about other media; they pay them to sell space. Although some media companies are now selling solutions, this is not universal in the industry. It should be of paramount importance for the media to educate their staff on the other media options and teach them how to listen and put together a suggested buy that is in the clients' best interests—not just theirs.

> Each medium has pros and cons and is highly contingent on the media rep. The media rep is your chef and can cook up a great plan for you if they listen and put together the right ingredients. Small business owners can ensure they have a first-rate chef by asking a few very simple questions:

> 1. Do you have three references that I can call that have done business with you in the past?

2. Do you have a case study of a business that is similar to mine that has used your station and been successful?
3. What things can I do in my advertising to make it measurable?
4. What makes your medium better than another medium?
5. What does $5,000 in your medium get me with your competitors from an audience standpoint?
6. Here is my target audience. Does your listener/viewer fit this profile? What percentage of your listeners/viewers is this profile?
7. What value-added opportunities to you offer? What events can I participate in and what dollar amount would that entail?
8. How long will you be on my account? Can you make decisions or do you have to go back to your boss?
9. How do you measure your audience and is that audience level guaranteed?
10. What if you make a mistake with my ad? Can I get a make-good?

TIP: Don't buy a station because you like the rep or because it's your favorite. And don't consider investing in any advertising or promotion with any station or publication unless you know it targets your desired audience.

These are just a few of the questions before you get into all the rates and other specifics. The first two questions are critical to see if your sales representative is going to be the right partner for you or just another commission-hungry sales animal.

TIP: Ask your radio and television reps to alert you in advance of special programs especially suited to your business so you can advertise within or immediately adjacent to them.

Most of the time you will get along with your media sales reps. If you should end up with a personality clash, call the station or publication manager and request a new salesperson. It happens. And most places will be more than happy to honor your request. Because nothing in life goes smoothly forever, avoid unpleasant situations down the road by keeping relationships with your media sales reps on a pleasant, but strictly business basis. It makes it a whole lot easier to deal with problems that may arise or to say no to that favorite salesperson from radio station A, a station you need, when he shows up selling radio station B, a station you do not need. When filled out properly, your worksheets will contain all of the decision-making information you need to say yes or no to any sales representative, taking it out of the personal arena altogether.

If your business is to succeed, *you* must be a great salesperson. Observe and listen to your media sales reps. You can learn a lot from the good ones who are great enough at what they do to do anything—and choose to be your media sales representative.

Chapter 7

Interns

I F YOU FIND YOURSELF WEARING TOO MANY HATS AND WITHOUT ADEQUATE funds to hire enough people to fill the demand, look to your local college and university intern programs for help. Many junior and senior students are waiting on lists in those programs for businesses in the community to give them a hands-on opportunity to use what they've learned. All it takes is a phone call and a few minutes to fill out a form giving some information about your business and stating the kind of intern you're looking for.

Interns can:

► Build your business web site.

► Put together media or marketing plans.

► Place advertising schedules.

► Write advertising copy.

► Do market research.

► Write and present sales proposals.

► Develop press releases.

► Study your competitors.

► Look for opportunities to promote your business.

► Explore ways to expand your customer base.

You can host students who will help in advertising, accounting, merchandising, purchasing, and marketing. You name it: if you need it, you can probably find an intern to help. But for help with your advertising and brand-building, your interns will probably come from the following major programs of study:

- ▶ Communication
- ▶ Advertising/Marketing
- ▶ Graphic Design
- ▶ Information Technology
- ▶ Computer Web Site Design
- ▶ International Business (depending on your company)

You, or the head of the department in which your intern will work, must have some expertise in the career field of the interns you plan to host. This is a *must* for supervision and evaluation purposes. In turn, you are providing a meaningful real-world work setting for someone who has learned a great deal from lectures and books, but needs hands-on experience. And the student will find it valuable to add this work to his or her résumé for subsequent job hunting.

The intern's work hours should suit both your business needs and his or her school schedule. At approximately midpoint in the semester, the sponsoring college or university will contact you regarding the intern's progress. While you may not be asked or required to pay a weekly salary (although some companies do pay interns on a voluntary basis), you will need to keep track of his or her hours and performance, as the student will receive a grade for the internship based on your reports.

Internships are commonplace at large companies and there is no reason small business owners should not take advantage of these great programs and reap the rewards.

Internships are a natural opportunity to scout out talent for permanent employment with your company. Many students look forward to such an offer and take internships very seriously, not only for a good grade, but for the possibility of a great reference or even a job. Even though each intern will be with you for only one semester, you can continue to be a part of the program and host a student year after year! Good for them … good for you!

Chapter 8

Co-op Advertising

C O-OP ADVERTISING IS A COOPERATIVE ADVERTISING EFFORT between a supplier and a retailer. Co-op is an opportunity for you to get some help with the cost of almost every form of advertising. If you are in retail sales, you will find that some of your suppliers have co-op money available for you if you advertise specific brands of merchandise. Many suppliers and franchise companies have programs in place that will pay up to 50 percent of your radio, television, outdoor, or print advertising. The amount you can expect to receive is based on a percentage of your orders, so look to your largest suppliers for help with co-op money, commercials, and print ads that are ready to go.

For example, if the amount you have available from ABS brand is $1,000 based on your purchases from that company, you can buy up to $2,000 of advertising and be reimbursed for half of it. Not all companies are as generous. Some will pay up to 25 percent, some less. But it's always worth asking about.

Your account executives should be able to help you determine what amounts of co-op money you have available and the deadlines for using it. Some think that it's not worth the trouble you go through to take advantage of co-op dollars and they would rather lose out on the money than deal with it. But it's not all that complicated. Your media reps will even have co-op books of participating manufacturers, listed alphabetically by brands, to locate those you can take advantage of.

Co-op is available for:

- ▶ Television
- ▶ Radio
- ▶ Outdoor
- ▶ Print
- ▶ Direct mail
- ▶ Some transit

Co-op does not cover:

- ▶ Production of any kind
- ▶ Radio or TV ads shorter than 30 seconds in length
- ▶ Agency costs
- ▶ Talent fees
- ▶ Dubs (copies of radio or television ads)

Once you determine what co-op dollars are available to you:

- ▶ Write separate contracts for each product or brand.
- ▶ Have your media reps write "co-op" and the appropriate brand name on all orders that apply. It will not only be proof that the advertising was indeed used for the correct brand (which will be part of the required paperwork), but if you are able to use co-op with more than one product, it will help you sort out paperwork at a later date.
- ▶ Keep copies of co-op claims in a folder.

Don't be put off if a supplier makes it sound complicated. Insist that all requirements be made clear at the outset. You can save a lot of money by persisting and your reps will gladly help, because it means you are able to spend more money on advertising than you might be able to do without co-op.

Figure 8-1 shows an example of the top section of a contract for co-op and the information you should be sure is on it to keep your paperwork straight when it's time to submit.

The first thing to do is to call the companies of the biggest brands you carry and ask for their co-op information. You will be sent paperwork that lays out all of the rules and regulations. Go over it with your media sales reps if you have questions, or just call the company and ask for clarification.

WXXX Contract

Client: P&P Bathroom Accessory Company

Contract #: 3333333

Schedule dates: May 15, 2005–October 3, 2005

Direct Advertiser ❑

Agency ❑

Co-op ❑

Brand: Furry seat covers

Check the box next to Direct Advertiser (if you are) and Co-op. Declare your brand.

Figure 8-1. Example of a co-op contract

There will be requirements, for any advertising you create on your own, to qualify for the co-op dollars. This can be as simple as adding in the brand's logo three times during a television spot, showing specific products, or including a sentence or two in radio spots.

For *radio* you will be asked to submit:

▶ A copy of your script(s) notarized by the radio station(s)

▶ A copy of your schedule(s) indicating brand notarized by the radio station(s)

▶ A copy of the produced spot(s) on a CD or cassette

For *TV* you will be asked to submit:

▶ A copy of your script(s) notarized by the TV station(s)

▶ A copy of your schedule(s) indicating brand notarized by the TV station(s)

▶ A copy of the produced spot(s) on VHS or CD

For *print* you will be asked to submit:

▶ A POP (proof of publication). This is a "tear sheet"—the entire page of the paper or publication your ad appears on. It shows the name of the publication and date. This will be sent to you by the publication along with your invoice.

▶ A copy of your invoice

For *outdoor* you will be asked to submit:

▶ A photo of the posted billboard design

▶ A copy of your invoice

How do you know if it's worth it to pursue co-op? This table shows the pros and cons of co-op.

Pros of using co-op	Cons of using co-op
▶ You can save up to 50 percent of some of your advertising costs. ▶ It's available for virtually every form of advertising. ▶ Your media reps will provide the paperwork and copies of your ads you need to submit. ▶ You have the ability to advertise more, which is critical in bringing people to your business.	▶ You can spend significant amounts of time managing it. ▶ Each form of advertising has its own rules and regulations for using co-op. ▶ You must stay completely organized.

Now you decide.

Chapter 9

Political Advertising

*I*F YOU'RE A POLITICIAN, FORGIVE ME. *POLITICAL ADS BENEFIT THOSE RUN-*ning for office in many ways. They get unlimited access to radio and television at a cheaper price than anyone else.

But for the small business owner, political ads are a nightmare. And, although you won't hear it said out loud (in public, anyway) by anyone who works at a radio or television station, they're a total nightmare for them as well.

Those of you who went through the pre-holiday advertising season along with the 2004 election already know what it's like to fight an 800-pound gorilla. It's the same with any election, but particularly with one that's hotly contested, whether it's a presidential race or a contest for governor, senator, sheriff, or mayor. Local ads can muck up inventory every bit as much as national ads.

During what many small business owners consider to be their most important advertising window, because of pre-holiday and holiday sales, political ads take over—literally—as local radio and television stations lose inventory to them.

Political ads are given special treatment in the following ways:

▶ They're charged the lowest per-spot rate that has been given to any paying client on that station for the previous 45 days. (It used to be for the previous year!)

▶ They're granted an automatic 15percent discount.

▶ They're given the status to preempt higher-cost, non-political paid advertisers if station inventory space runs low.

Law dictates this. Radio and television stations have no say whatsoever. They *must* run political ads, even at the expense of paid advertising by non-political clients. No one wins except the politicians.

▶ The small business owner suffers because of the disruption to his or her pre-holiday and holiday sale ads that are often preempted by political ads during September, October, and early November.

▶ The stations suffer because the onslaught of low-rate political ads replaces normal revenue.

▶ The sales reps, who are paid on commission, suffer with smaller pay-checks.

During the political window that runs from about July 19 to Election Day, the law prohibits anything called "value-added" to be offered to advertisers. So if your rep promises to give you "free spins" during that period of time, know that it's illegal.

The only way for stations to avoid the political advertising problem is to refuse to accept even one political ad. Once they accept one, they must accept all. This is an enormous headache for the radio and television industries as well as a loss of scheduled advertising for small business owners who have placed their hard-earned advertising dollars, hoping that the ads will draw customers to their stores during the prime holiday shopping period.

On the other hand, for stations with little business during the year, political advertising is a real boon. But you wouldn't be on those stations anyway, right? Right? *Right?*

Here are some tips:

▶ Don't try to run any trade advertising during this time. Trade (providing product or services in lieu of cash for advertising costs) is preemptable anyway under normal circumstances, so you can just kiss this goodbye when political ads are in full swing.

▶ Use other methods of advertising, like newspapers, direct mail, outdoor billboards, or transit advertising. Your ads will still be competing for attention with all of the commotion, but at least they won't get "bumped" from these forms of advertising.

▶ If you really are desperate for TV, try cable. There's a lot more space to sell and your sales rep will be able to get you in somewhere on a cable station that reaches your target audience. Cable stations will also be inundated with political advertisers and you will find that even some of those stations will be unavailable to you.

▶ Early schedule placement doesn't help. If your space is needed, you'll get bumped.

Chapter 10

Radio

EVEN IF YOU LIVE IN A MEDIUM-SIZE MARKET, THERE CAN BE MORE THAN 30 radio stations willing to sell you advertising time. This sounds like a bad thing, I know, but it's not as hard to determine which stations will be right for you as it seems at the outset. Why? Because each station has a very specific audience to deliver and not all of them will match your desired demographic needs. Radio is one of the easiest, fastest, and most powerful forms of advertising available—as long as you know which stations in your market are best suited to your customers or clients.

Demographics

First, pay no attention to reports in your local newspapers, or anywhere else, that rank local radio stations using 12+ as a demographic. There is no one station that will appeal to everyone over the age of 12. To find the right station or stations to use for your business, you must be very specific as to age and gender groups. Use only the choices you made from demographic groups A and B in the beginning of this book—and you'll notice there is no 12+ choice—as your guide for your radio purchases.

Radio targets specific populations divided into groups by age and gender. Once you know who your customers are, you will be able to pinpoint the stations that will deliver your message directly to them. Most stations

Geography

Radio stations cover different geographic areas. By looking at a coverage map, you can determine if a radio station will be beneficial for your business location(s).

Some maps will show two circles to indicate their strongest and weakest areas of coverage as you can see in the examples below.

The smallest circles show the strongest coverage areas, Metro Survey Areas (MSAs). In these areas, people should receive these stations clearly on almost any radio.

Between the first and second largest circles is the TSA (Total Survey Area). The station's signal may be weak here unless you have a really good car radio or stereo and you may need an antenna.

You should not consider the station if your locations are outside of the second circle, referred to as "fringe."

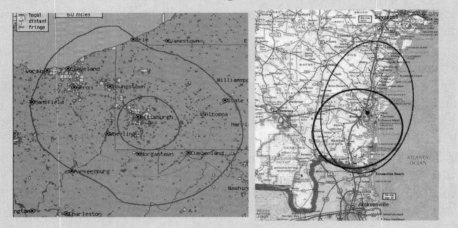

Figure 10-1. Examples of a radio coverage map

have a primary and a secondary audience. However, the secondary group can be very small and not worth the price of advertising. While expert media buyers are able to spend not only hours, but days and weeks, dissecting primary and secondary audiences, it is in your best interest to simplify the options and choose stations according to their primary strengths. You will probably find two to six radio stations in your market with the right audience for your business. When several appropriate stations are available to you, one of them will have the lion's share of listeners and be the most expensive. There is nothing wrong with using the #2 or even the #3 station—if one exists—as long as the audience is made up of the demographic group you need. The rule of thumb is now, and will always be, that the larger the audience, the more expensive the station will be to use.

Stations with different formats have audiences with different listening habits and you will need to incorporate this information into your buying decisions. Beautiful music, soft rock, talk radio, and country music have audiences that listen the longest, while most other formats have younger listeners who flip through stations in search of their favorite tunes. When you use a station where the audience listens for long periods of time, you can use fewer commercials than you can with a station catering to "channel surfers."

There will also be some audience crossover between stations with similar formats or even stations with different formats that cater to the same demographic groups. In other words, a baby boomer might listen to talk radio during the week and switch to a station broadcasting what is often known as "golden oldies" in the evenings and on weekends. They are crossing over from one station to another, so by advertising on just one of those stations, you are able to reach a portion of the second audience as well.

Depending on your product or service, you may decide to use *tactical* advertising—running a large number of commercials for a short period of time—or *strategic* (or "maintenance") advertising—running a smaller schedule over a long period of time.

A store selling major appliances would use strategic advertising, because major appliances don't break down every day. This type of store needs to create name awareness in the minds of the public so that when a potential customer needs to buy a new washing machine he or she will think of that store as the first place to go. Telling the public, "This weekend you can save 25 percent on washing machines" works only for those people who need to buy one now—a very small percent of those who will need one eventually.

However, a store that wants to sell 500 plants on a given weekend will use tactical advertising and buy a large amount of commercials in a four- or five-day period leading up to and including the sale weekend.

On an FM radio station, there are on average eight openings per hour from 5 A.M. to midnight every day and 10 openings for the same period of time on an AM station. (Average because you will find a few less per hour from 5 A.M. to 9 A.M. and a few more openings per hour from 9 A.M. to midnight.) Using X as one commercial, I lined up 152 spot openings per day on an FM station and 190 per day on an AM station. 190 Xs looks like this:

58

xxxx**X**xxxxxxxxxxxxxxxxxxxxxxxxxxxxxxxxxxxxxxxxx**X**xxxxxxxxxxxxxxx
xxxxxxxxxxxxxxxxxxxxxxxxxxxxxxxxxxxxxxxxxx**X**xxxxxxxxxxxxxxxxxxxxxxx
xxxxxxxxxxxxxxxxxxxxx**X**xxxxxxxxxxxxxxxxxxx**X**xxxxxxxxxxxxxxxxxxxxx

The five larger X's were added to represent your five spots, so you can see how many other commercials you would be competing against that day.

Let's say you were going to run five spots a day for one week. The 35 X's show what your message must break through when you place that number of commercials during one week.

xxxxxxxxxxxxxxxxxxxxxxx**X**xxxxxxxxxxxxxxxxxxxxxxxxxxxxxxxxxxx**X**xxxx
xxxxxxxxxxxxxxxxxxxxxxxx**X**xxxxxxxxxxxxxxxxxxxxxxxxxxxxxxxxxxxxxxxxxx
xxxxxxxxxxxxxxxxxxxxx**X**xxxxx**X**xxxxxxxxxxxxxxxxxxxxxxxxxxxxxxxxxxx**X**
xxxxxxxxxxxxxxxxxxxxxxxxxxxxxxxxxxxxxxxxxxxxxxxxxx**X**xxxxxx

xxxxxxxxxxxxxxxxxxxxxxxxxxxx**X**xxxxxxxxxxxxxxxxxxxxxxxxxxxxxxxxxxx
xxxxxxxxxxxxxxxxxxx**X**xxxxxxxxxxxxxxxxxxxxxxxxxxxxxxxxxxxxxxxxxxxxxx
Xxxxxxxxxxxxxx**X**xxxxxxxxxxxxxxxxxxxxxxxxxxxxxx**X**xxxxxxxxxxxxxxx
xxxxxxxxxxxxxxxxxxxxxxxxxxxxxxxx**X**xxxxxxxxxxxxxxxxxxxxxxxxxxx

xxxxxxxxxxxxxxxxxxxxxxx**X**xxxxxxxxxx**X**xxxxxxxxxxxxxxxxxxxxxxxxxx
xxx**X**xxxxxxxxxxxxxxxxxxx**X**xxxxxxxxxxxxxxxxxxxxxxxxxxxxxxxxxxxxxx
xxxxxx**X**xxxxxxxxxxxxxxxxxxxxxxxxxxxxxxxxxxxxxxxxxxxxxxxxxxxxxxx**X**
xxxx**X**xxxxxxxxxxxxxxxxxxxxxxxxxx**X**xxxxxxxxxxxxxxxxxxxxxxxx
xxxxxxxxxxxxxxxxxxxxxxxxxxx**X**xxxxxxxxxxxxxxxxxxxxxxxxxxxxxxxx
xxxxxxxxx**X**xxxxxxxxxxxxxxxxxxxxxxxxxxxxxxxxxxxxxxxxxxxxxxxxxxx

xxx**X**xxxxxxxxxxxxxxxxxxxxxxxxxxxxxxxxxxxx**X**xxxxxxxxx**X**xxxxxxx
xxxxxxxxxxxxxxxxxxxxxxxxxxxxxxxxxxxxxxxxxxxxx**X**xxxxxxxxxxx
Xxxxxxxxxxxxx**X**xxxxxxxxxxxxxxxxxxxxxxxxxxxxxxxxxxxxxxxxxxxxxx
xxxxxxxxxxxxxxxxxxxxxxxxxxxxxxxxxxx**X**xxxxxxxxxxxxxxxxxxxxxxxx**X**
xxxxxxxxxxxxxxxxxxxxxxxxxxxxxxxxxxxxxxxxxxxxxxxxxxxxxxxxxxxxx
xxxxxxxxxxxxxxxxxxxxxxxxxxxxxx**X**xxxxxxxxxxxxxxxxxxxxxxxxxxxxx**X**xx
xxxxxxxxxxxxxxxxxxxxx**X**xxxxxxxxxxxxxxxxxxxxxxxxxxxxxxxxxx**X**xxxxxx

This is what scares people about buying radio ads. It seems that you have to buy hundreds of spots a week to be heard. Luckily, you don't need a lot of these X's to have a good advertising schedule. You just need to know which X's you need and which you don't to place your advertising efficiently, because different people and different *numbers* of people listen to radio at different times of the day and night.

Dayparts

At most stations, "morning drive" Monday through Friday is the most expensive, "after-noon drive" is next, "mid-day" is next, and "evening" is the least expensive.

An essential concept for radio advertising is *daypart*. Radio broadcast time is divided into chunks, usually about four or five hours long, according to listening patterns. Each block of time is a daypart and each varies in advertising cost.

At most stations, "morning drive" Monday through Friday is the most expensive, "afternoon drive" is next, "mid-day" is next, and "evening" is the least expensive. Weekends are usually less than weekdays and you can pay next to nothing to advertise overnight between midnight and 5 A.M., but your audience is severely reduced. However, if you are in an area where factories and hospitals require a lot of shift work, you may actually see a little response from overnight.

Let's take another look at the section of X's above. Let's say that the top (shaded) portion represents morning drive. The next (not shaded) portion represents midday, the next (shaded) portion is afternoon drive, and the last (not shaded) area is evening. And let's pretend that this station's audience is made up of women.

Are you looking for an audience of working women ages 25-54? Then you can concentrate your 35 commercials into morning and afternoon drive times (shaded areas). This cuts way down on the spread of your commercials and enables you to reach more women with your message, right? Similarly, if you are trying to reach stay-at-home women 25-54 or women in that age group who work from home, you can concentrate your spots into mid-day.

Sometimes a station turns to a different format for the evening daypart. This one, for example, may air a show for teenagers to call in and talk about problems. If you want to advertise to the young teen girl, concentrate your spots into evening. Before you buy, you must ask your reps if their stations change format at any time during the day or evening.

An all-day schedule is called a Total Audience Plan (TAP) and is designed to run throughout all dayparts for a slightly lower rate. A TAP reaches listeners morning, noon, and night, giving your message a chance to be heard by all of the different people who listen to that station during every part of the day.

Commercial Length

Most radio stations sell "units" rather than 30- or 60-second spots. Units are defined as the number of different messages a listener hears in any commercial break. In other words, a commercial break of three minutes can hold six 30-second spots or three 60-second spots. A listener will perceive the three 60-second spots as "only" three commercials but might become annoyed at listening to six different 30-second spots—even though the commercial time is the same. Radio stations switched to unit pricing primarily because they wanted to have their listeners perceive as few commercials as possible and because they knew that most advertisers would choose :60s over :30s.

Because of this leaning toward selling units, you are able to purchase a 60-second spot for the same price as a 30-second spot. You may be wondering, Why would anyone choose a :30 when they can have a :60 for the same price? National chains, manufacturers with co-op spots, and franchises providing advertising support, for example, sometimes produce their spots in a 30-second format. Also, some stations attach 30-second spots to their sponsorship packages of news, sports, weather, or traffic.

While some people in radio sales are of the opinion that 60 seconds' worth of any commercial message is boring to the listening audience, you should make that determination yourself. When I am developing a commercial, I will always use 60 seconds if the prices are the same. I like having more time to repeat important facts and dates, being more creative with copy, and hammering away at the business name and location. Getting copywriting help from creative reps will help keep your material interesting for the listeners.

While some people in radio sales are of the opinion that 60 seconds' worth of any commercial message is boring to the listening audience, you should make that determination yourself.

Whichever length of commercial you decide to use, ask your reps for the best possible rate. Then when you call to actually place an order, ask if they can do even better. Don't be afraid to let your reps know you are calling around to get the best deal possible.

Sponsorships

A popular way to make the most of a low-frequency schedule is to purchase a *sponsorship*. This means purchasing the right to have your business credited with bringing the news, sports, weather, traffic reports, etc., to the listening audience. This sponsoring is done with identifying *billboards or sponsor IDs,* which state, for example, "This edition of the news is brought to you by the P&P Bathroom Accessory Company." Along with the identifying billboard, the business receives a 30- or 60-second commercial within close proximity to the report.

Sponsorships are usually purchased on long-term contracts, meaning at least 13 weeks, often 26 or 52 weeks. You can purchase a sponsorship for two to five days per week, depending on your budget. Week in and week out, your company is credited with your chosen report(s) and the audience gets used to hearing your name.

Commercials accompanying a news, weather, traffic, or sports report receive more attention than commercials plugged into musical sequences. Because the audience is listening for specific information and is paying close attention to these reports, it is said to be in a *listening mode*.

Along the same lines, it can be argued that commercials placed in radio talk shows are heard more readily. Listeners pay attention to large segments of this format because they are interested in the subject matter or enjoy listening to a popular show host. They are also in a listening mode.

If you can afford a low-frequency 52-week sponsorship and also be able to add higher-frequency schedules several times a year for sales or special events, you're in a good position to increase sales and name awareness.

Commercials accompanying a news, weather, traffic, or sports report receive more attention than commercials plugged into musical sequences.

Combos

Your radio salesperson may represent two or more stations—combinations of AM and FM stations owned by the same company, very often with studios and offices in the same building. You can take advantage of a lower "combo rate" if you are willing to buy time on two or more of these stations instead of just one. Be sure any stations you combine meet your demographic requirements.

No matter how many stations are owned by one entity, you will usually not find a radio salesperson representing more than two of the stations at a time. The only exceptions are when special packages show up at the beginning of the year or with promotions during the year that include all of the stations (like the example below), where one sales rep can handle the deal for you.

Example: Clear Channel offers a summer web site promotion called "One Tank Trips" that I buy for my amusement park client every year. It includes promotions on their seven local radio stations that talk about places people go during the summer on no more than one tank of gasoline. The promotions point listeners to a web site that lists my client and others, with links to their web sites. One salesperson handles that purchase for me, even though seven stations are involved.

Keith Alper, CEO of Creative Producers Group, Inc. in St. Louis, Missouri (*www.getcreative.com*), says:

> For small and medium-sized businesses, times have changed as more media companies (i.e., Infinity, Clear Channel, etc.) have consolidated. For some it may mean fewer buying opportunities and less competition. For others, it's actually resulted in better packages, and better deals.
>
> ▶ Demand some type of promotion package be included in your radio buys, like a remote or tickets to something. These cost the stations nothing and can increase the effectiveness of your buy/offering.
>
> ▶ Meet media management (General Sales Manager or the head of sales). They have the ability to give you the best buy, promotions, etc. Media property account executives come and go as though through a revolving door.
>
> ▶ Some stations or media properties will let you "test" a campaign with them with special terms. If you can find one, this can be a win-win situation. But these stations are rare.
>
> ▶ Test, test, test. Discover what works best for your limited ad and/or promotions budget. Print? Online? Cable? Radio? Does a blend work best? Or just buying heavily in one media?
>
> ▶ What are your competitors doing? Sometimes the best way to find out is to go directly to the media outlet. While you may not get all of the details, they can be helpful.
>
> ▶ Explore other media outlets. Sometimes there are hidden gems … small niche radio stations, neighborhood newspapers, community centers, etc. If targeted correctly there is less clutter, less expense, and you become a big client to them.

Tom Matzell, President and Creative Director of MRW Communications in Boston (*www.mrwinc.com*), says:

> If your budget is limited (whose isn't?), stick to one or two media that you can afford to saturate. Spreading your dollars too thin over all media waters down the effectiveness of your campaign.
>
> A good example is a small furniture store in the Boston area that decided to make radio its primary vehicle. They did so with a vengeance, buying up as much airtime as they could and delivering a consistent message. They never fell into the "I tried radio for a week and it didn't work" syndrome. They made a six-month commitment and stuck to it. The rest is history. Today they are one of the largest chains in the country and the most profitable per-square-foot furniture stores anywhere. Local radio (and now TV, too) is still their mainstay.

Promotions

A promotion is a form of advertising designed to bring extra impact to a special event. A promotion is a *happening,* over and above usual advertising. For example, if a bookstore runs a sale of 20 percent off everything in the store, it's normal advertising. If the store is offering 20 percent off a new bestseller, has the author on the premises to sign copies, and perhaps even runs a contest to have dinner with the author, it's a promotion. Your budget will dictate whether you can engage in a promotion with one station or with several.

A radio station may come to you looking for participants for a promotional event it has cooked up and in need of prizes for on-air giveaways. But don't wait for that. If you have an idea for a promotion, get your rep(s) interested in participating in your special event. Outline the details, specify the budget you are prepared to expend, and ask what they can offer in the way of sign-up-to-win entry boxes, signage, appearances by one or more of their personalities, or remotes (having one of the personalities broadcast from your location on the day of your event). Your budget, the right station(s), and the excitement you create with your advertising will pretty much determine the success or failure of your promotion.

Your budget, the right station(s), and the excitement you create with your advertising will pretty much determine the success or failure of your promotion.

When participating in this type of station event, ask for promotional announcements to accompany your advertising schedule. This means that every time the upcoming event is promoted, your business will be mentioned. Most promotions are heavily scheduled through the week preceding the event; these promotional mentions mean your business name will be heard over and over again. When a station's personality is going to make a personal appearance at your event, you can be sure you will receive plenty of promotional mentions during his or her show. When lots of people show up at an event, it can be an indication of the popularity of the station and the personality in the market, so they will do what they can to get people there.

It needs to be mentioned here that Mother Nature has been known to defeat the most carefully planned event. If you're going to be outside or if people need to travel any distance to take part, the weather can be a maker or a breaker. Depending on your location and the time of year, you may lose the day to excessive heat, humidity, rain, blizzards, windstorms, or hazardous road conditions.

Trade Advertising

Trade advertising is just what it sounds like: you trade product or service for the cost of advertising. For example, you run a $2,000 advertising schedule on a particular radio station and, instead of paying cash, you provide the same dollar amount in products or services to that station. Radio stations have needs for products and services that they don't particularly want to spend cash for either. They need products and services for on-air contests such as get-away vacations, visits to spas, home improvements, florists, tickets to movies, concerts or plays, gift certificates to restaurants, and general merchandise. And they need products and services for their own use, such as automobiles (and maintenance for those vehicles, like cleaning, tires, etc.), office furniture, office machines, janitorial and decorating services, paper products, printing, catering services, party facilities, landscaping, and more. They will be eager to trade advertising for what they need, so don't hesitate to contact appropriate stations and ask about trade advertising.

Once in a great while you can work a 100 percent trade, but what is more common is an agreement consisting of half cash/half trade, allowing that 50 percent of your advertising is paid in cash and the other 50 percent is taken in merchandise or services from your business.

When participating in trade advertising, use your retail price or full service hourly rate to figure the dollar amount and always think of it as cash.

When participating in trade advertising, use your retail price or full service hourly rate to figure the dollar amount and always think of it as cash. Most stations will want you to sign a contract stating that the trade portion of your advertising is preemptable. That is, if enough paying customers are available to buy the air space promised to you, the station will bump your trade ad in favor of the cash customer and run your ad when space again becomes available. Always try to negotiate that preempt clause from the contract. You will have the most luck with this in the first and third quarters, when demand for airtime is not so high and, of course, when there is naturally less chance of getting bumped.

The single most important consideration in deciding to participate in trade advertising is whether the station can provide you with the audience you need. If a station cannot deliver the audience you need, do not participate, no matter how great it sounds! Trade can be tempting because not all of the advertising is paid in cash. But advertising on a station you would not otherwise use is wasting the value of the merchandise or the services you give away. Consider the cost of your merchandise or services as cash and part with it just as carefully.

Trade and promotion advertising are creative ways of adding impact to your advertising projects. Tell your sales people you are interested and to keep you in mind when opportunities arise.

Frequency

Correct radio schedule frequencies can be complicated to determine. If you would like to take the time to gather, dissect, and calculate extensive amounts of Arbitron information, here are some definitions and equations you can use. Don't feel badly if you don't want to do this; you don't really need to. Your completed radio worksheets will give you all the information you need to conduct an accurate, targeted, no-nonsense advertising program. However, perusing the following equations will show you why advertising is a full-time job for those who love it. You will also see how valuable the worksheets in this book are and how much time and money they save you when it's time to promote your business.

Average Quarter-Hour (AQH) Persons: The average number of people listening to one station for at least five minutes out of a given 15-minute period. You can get these numbers from your rep(s).

Average Quarter-Hour Rating: The AQH estimate shown as a percent of the sampled population. You can ask your sales rep for this figure in the Metro Survey Area (MSA) or the Total Survey Area (TSA). Both MSA and TSA are defined with the sample coverage maps earlier in this chapter. Here's the equation you use to determine this figure:

$$\frac{AQH\ persons}{population} \times 100 = AQH\ rating\ (\%)$$

Cume Persons: The total number of different people who listen to one radio station for a minimum of five minutes during any one daypart (out of four dayparts: morning, midday, afternoon, and evening).

Cume Rating: The total number of different people (Cume persons) shown as a percent of the estimated population of a specific demographic group.

$$\frac{cume\ persons}{population} \times 100 = cume\ rating\ (\%)$$

Rating: The audience shown as a percent of the total population.

$$\frac{listeners}{population} \times 100 = rating\ (\%)$$

Share: The percent of all people listening to radio in general in the MSA who are tuned in to one particular station.

$$\frac{\text{AQH persons of one station}}{\text{AQH persons of all stations}} \times 100 = \text{share (\%)}$$

Gross Impressions (GIs): The total audience of AQH persons available for the total number of commercials in any given schedule.

$$\text{AQH persons} \times \text{number of commercials in a given schedule} = \text{GIs}$$

Gross Rating Points (GRPs): The total of all rating points gained for a given schedule.

$$\text{AQH rating} \times \text{number of commercials in a given schedule} = \text{GRPs}$$

Cost per rating point: The cost of reaching the AQH listening audience equal to 1 percent of the population in any one demographic group. This can be calculated in two ways:

$$\frac{\text{cost of schedule}}{\text{GRP}} = \text{cost per rating point}$$

$$\frac{\text{average cost per spot}}{\text{AQH rating}} = \text{cost per rating point}$$

Cost per thousand (CPM): The price of delivering 1,000 gross impressions. This can also be calculated in two ways:

Price of schedule

gross impressions x 1,000 = CPM

Spot cost

AQH persons x 1,000 = CPM

Frequency: The average number of times a person has the opportunity to hear a commercial.

$$\frac{\text{gross impressions}}{\text{net reach}} = \text{frequency}$$

You can get the numbers you need for these equations only from a radio rep whose station subscribes to Arbitron. Those that do not subscribe are not allowed *under any circumstances* to use or supply specific Arbitron numbers to clients or to use Arbitron numbers in making a pitch for their station or against another station. Most radio stations do subscribe and will be happy to furnish you with whatever numbers you need to do the math. Your radio account executive(s) will be happy to go through the steps with you.

Contracts

Most stations offer discounts for long term, *consecutive week* contracts—usually 5 percent for a 26-week contract and 10 percent for a 52-week contract. Not only are discounts offered for *long-term* contracts, but also you will receive a price break for *high-frequency* schedules. For example, you will pay less per commercial (spot) when you run 18 of them in one week than you would pay per spot for a 12X per week schedule. And you will pay less per spot for running 24X per week than you would for 18X.

Generally, 24X-35X is the most you would ever need to purchase in one week on any one station. At that point, added frequency can inch you toward the point of diminishing returns where you find yourself spending money unnecessarily—in short, overkill.

If you have the budget to run 24-35 commercials each week, do it. Don't hold back to see what will happen if you only run 12 commercials. As you've always heard with buying real estate, the number-1 consideration is location, location, location. The same thing applies when buying radio, but add frequency, frequency, frequency to the saying. Always run as many commercials as you can afford and never run more than you can afford.

Radio rate sheets are called "wish lists" largely because the printed rates are the ones the stations wish they could get. Remember that the rule of thumb is that the stations with the largest audiences are the stations with the highest rates. When a station rep comes to you with a sales pitch of "buy one commercial, get one commercial free," it may mean that the station has a lot of unsold inventory—maybe because it's the first quarter, when all stations can use business, or maybe it's because the station has few listeners and can be generous in hopes of getting your business.

In reality, you can negotiate a lower rate than the ones shown on any rate sheet, especially during first quarter when advertising is always down and it's possible to negotiate a great annual contract and enjoy the lower rates all year long.

Generally, 24X-35X is the most you would ever need to purchase in one week on any one station.

When to Change Horses

When a station changes to a new format, you will need to have your worksheets updated to reflect its new expected audience. A new format needs time to settle into the community and take root with its new audience. If you have a contract with a radio station and that station changes its format, you not only have the ability to cancel your contract immediately, but you *should* do so immediately. Even if the new format is expected to have the same demographic profile as the old one, it will take time for people to get used it and decide if they want to keep listening there or move on to another station. Your rep(s) should notify you as soon as any major change is made—even before the change occurs, if possible. If you keep your completed worksheets, as suggested, you can quickly call a rep from another appropriate station and continue your advertising.

Annual Packages

At the beginning of every year, you'll have the opportunity to purchase an annual contract at a discounted rate. You can:

- ► Commit to running a specific number of spots per month over the year.
- ► Commit to running a specific number of spots during certain weeks or months throughout the year that would coincide with sales or special events you've planned in advance.
- ► Commit to a sponsorship for either a full year or for certain periods of time throughout the year.
- ► Commit to a specific number of spots with no real plan in mind as to when you'll use them. This is the most difficult to manage, as you may find that when you decide to run some of the spots, the space you want is already sold out. You must still find the time to run the spots you signed up for before the end of your contract.

Sometimes your radio account executives will offer you a specific package at the beginning of the year that includes a large number of stations (owned by one entity) at a discounted rate. Do not commit to one of these packages if any of the stations are ones you would not buy on their own merits. These packages are designed to force people to buy stinky stations—stinky either because they do not reach your target audience or because they have no audience and they can't push them off on anyone. The packages carry a per-spot cost that is so low you might think it's worth having the junky stations in the mix. That is the smoke-and-mirrors part of the game.

Here's how it works. Your radio rep comes to you with a package that would include six stations. We'll call them:

Station A—a station you could use

Station B—a station you would not use

Station C—a station you would not use

Station D—a station you could use

Station E—a station you would not use

Station F—a station you would not use

In this package you would receive 30 spots on each station, *one week a month for the year*. You'd be getting 180 spots (30 on each station) during each week you run, over the course of the year (12 total weeks). So you would receive a total of 2,160 spots at $17 each. Your total annual (12 week) schedule would run you $36,720.

Now look at the actual rates for each individual station:

Station A—a station you could use (sold at $45 per spot)

Station B—a station you would never use (sold at $3 per spot—no audience)

Station C—a station you would never use (sold at $10 per spot—doesn't hit your target)

Station D—a station you could use (sold at $30 per spot)

Station E—a station you would never use (sold at $8 per spot—no audience)

Station F—a station you would never use (sold at $6 per spot—doesn't hit your target)

If, instead, you run on only the two stations that you could actually use to reach your target market, at their regular per-spot cost, you would spend $27,000—and probably less, since you could negotiate down the rate on each station by at least 10 percent.

So, with the full package with the $17 rate, you would actually spend $9,720 for the spots that would run on stations with no audience or that did not hit your target audience. *Money wasted!* But you would be thinking that you were getting a deal because you were paying only $17 a spot. Not so. Your invoices (should you inspect them closely) would indicate that you were paying the rates shown above for each station—and that the rates had been averaged out to get that $17 rate to show you during the sale.

Summertime, Summertime, Sum, Sum, Summertime!

Repeats on television, kids and teachers on vacation, people taking time off from work, travelers making their way to beaches, amusement parks, camping trips—all make radio the perfect medium for advertisers during the summer months. Even with CDs and the onset of satellite radio, so far people can't zap commercials with a remote control in the car. Radio is great all year long, but in the summer it has a distinct edge. Don't miss the boat here: use radio to capture people in their cars, on the beach, and during their leisure hours.

Radio is great all year long, but in the summer it has a distinct edge.

Worksheets

Four times a year, radio stations are ranked by the survey company Arbitron and they are willing to pay large sums of money to secure the resulting information. When touting the benefits of a radio station, your sales reps may refer to the "numbers in the last book." They are referring to the station's position compared with all of the other radio stations in the same market as determined by the latest survey information. Four surveys a year result in four "books" a year—summer, fall, winter, and spring. Each book indicates the rise or fall of each station's ranking from the previous book.

In any one book there are many kinds of information. Reach and frequency answers two basic questions: *reach* = how many *different people* hear your commercial at least one time during your schedule and *frequency* = how many times *each unduplicated person* hears the spot. Current wisdom says a listener needs to hear a spot 2.5 times before he or she will act on it. The average time spent listening determines to some extent how many commercials you need to run on any single station to achieve that magic 2.5 number. Does the station's format hold the audience for long periods of time? Or is it a station with "channel surfers"? Therefore, the number of spots you run is just as important as choosing the correct station.

Think of each radio station as a building with a revolving door; inside each building, your commercials are playing on loudspeakers. At some stations, people come through the revolving doors and stay in the building a long time. At other stations, people come in and linger for just a short time. And at other stations, people just go around and around inside the revolving door and never really enter the building at all.

TIP: Start advertising your seasonal business earlier than you normally would, to increase name awareness and "mind-share" over your competitors.

It makes sense that you would need to run your commercial fewer times over the loudspeaker for the people who stay inside the building the longest. And it's reasonable to think that you would have to run the commercial a little more often for the people who only lingered for a while. And logical that you would have to play the commercial almost constantly for the people in the revolving door.

Your radio sales reps can help you determine how many commercials you need to run to be sure your schedule has the best chance of succeeding.

Directions for Worksheet #1

Worksheet #1 is for radio demographic rankings. Go through both pages and circle only the headings that coincide with the choices you made from Groups A and B in Chapter 5. Then give a copy to each radio sales rep to complete.

This worksheet will provide you with a list of the top four stations catering to the audience(s) you need. Keep the appropriate ones for future use. Because there are four books each year, have the sheets updated after each book to keep current.

Because the account executives know that you're giving these worksheets to everyone who calls on you, each will put the stations in the correct order even if it doesn't make his or her station(s) look so good. You should expect that all sheets will come back with the same four stations listed in the same order.

Keep in mind that Arbitron ratings are about audience *estimates*. Many advertisers like to look at the trends over three or four consecutive books. Every now and then an aberrant book turns up and a station with low ratings suddenly leaps to new heights without having changed its format, its personalities, or anything else. In other words, without any apparent reason. At the same time, it is possible for the opposite to happen when a strong station takes a dive. It is wise to wait until the *next* book comes out to see if the ratings stay the same or show more normal results. Usually, a drastic rise or fall of any one station that has had no major change is due to a "bad book" in which a true reading could not be obtained.

Radio Demographic Rankings

Worksheet #1

Station: _____ **Date:** _____

Circle the same choices below from Groups A and B as you did in Chapter 1. Have your radio rep(s) fill out *only the sections that match those selections.* This worksheet, when completed by your reps, will indicate how the top four stations reaching your desired audience(s) compare with each other. The information will be excerpted from research companies such as Arbitron and Nielsen and represents the most accurate data available.

GROUP A (age)	GROUP B (gender)
18-34	Female
18-49	Male
25-54	Adults (both male and female)
45+	

Source _____

Note to Rep: Please use average persons (00)

Market: Total Survey Area

Monday-Friday 5:30 A.M.-7 P.M.

Women 18-34	Men 18-34	Adults 18-34
1. _____	_____	_____
2. _____	_____	_____
3. _____	_____	_____
4. _____	_____	_____

Women 18-49	Men 18-49	Adults 18-49
1. _____	_____	_____
2. _____	_____	_____
3. _____	_____	_____
4. _____	_____	_____

Women 25-54	Men 25-54	Adults 25-54
1. _____	_____	_____
2. _____	_____	_____
3. _____	_____	_____
4. _____	_____	_____

continued on next page

	Women 45+	Men 45+	Adults 45+
1.	_____	_____	_____
2.	_____	_____	_____
3.	_____	_____	_____
4.	_____	_____	_____

Saturday-Sunday 9 A.M.-Midnight

	Women 18-34	Men 18-34	Adults 18-34
1.	_____	_____	_____
2.	_____	_____	_____
3.	_____	_____	_____
4.	_____	_____	_____

	Women 18-49	Men 18-49	Adults 18-49
1.	_____	_____	_____
2.	_____	_____	_____
3.	_____	_____	_____
4.	_____	_____	_____

	Women 25-54	Men 25-54	Adults 25-54
1.	_____	_____	_____
2.	_____	_____	_____
3.	_____	_____	_____
4.	_____	_____	_____

	Women 45+	Men 45+	Adults 45+
1.	_____	_____	_____
2.	_____	_____	_____
3.	_____	_____	_____
4.	_____	_____	_____

Notes:

_____

_____

_____

_____

_____

_____

Submitted by: _____ _____ _____

Name of Salesperson   Station   Date

Phone: _____ Fax: _____ E-mail: _____

Worksheet #2

Directions

Give both pages of Worksheet #2 *only* to the account executives who represent the four stations from Worksheet #1—the top stations that reach your target audience.

The first page of Worksheet #2 provides a general overview of a radio station—current information regarding its audience, prices, and available sponsorships.

Using X = 1 commercial, you can see how a schedule of 12 commercials, 18 commercials, or 24 commercials per week would be placed both during the week and on weekends. (Weekend schedules often include Friday.)

Example: The first sample schedule on the second page of Worksheet #2 shows 12 spots airing Monday through Friday. The commercials would be placed as follows: (3X) 5:30 A.M.-10 A.M., (3X) 10 A.M.-3 P.M., (3X) 3 P.M.- 7 P.M., (3X) 7 P.M.-10 P.M.

This means that during the five-day period, three of your commercials will run between 5:30 A.M. and 10 A.M. (morning drive), three will run between 10 A.M. and 3 P.M. (mid-day), three will run between 3 P.M. and 7 P.M. (afternoon drive), and three will run in the evening between 7 P.M. and midnight. Feel free to mold the hours to where you really want them, perhaps with a 7 A.M. start and a 10 P.M. cutoff.

The second page of Worksheet #2 is for scheduling ads.

When do you need to bolster business? While some businesses such as garden shops and theme parks may want to build weekend traffic, diet companies often like to advertise on Mondays because most people start diets on that day. Many restaurants want to build mid-week lunch traffic, while other businesses want to advertise all during the week.

Whether you need to increase business during the early portion of the week, at mid-week, on the weekends, or all week long, there are samples of properly placed schedules shown on the second page of Worksheet #2. These examples of radio schedules with different frequencies are designed to bolster your business at various times of the week.

When completed by your account executives, both pages will show for each station the costs of a 12X schedule, an 18X schedule, and a 24X schedule, which are all classic frequencies, and the cost of news, sports, traffic, or weather sponsorships. This will make it very easy for you to find a schedule at a glance and to place it with just a phone call to your rep.

RADIO WORKSHEET #2
Have Your Reps Fill Out and Return This Sheet

Radio Station Information	Call Letters _____ Dial Position _____
	Rep's Name _____
	Phone # _____ E-mail _____
	Format _____

Demographic Strength	Sales Rep: Circle the choices from Groups A and B that best describe your station's primary strength.

	Group A (age)	**Group B (gender)**
	18-34	Female
	18-49	Male
	25-54	Adults
	45+	

*Cost per week based on frequency of 12X, 18X, 24X, Monday–Friday 5:30A–Midnight

(:60 sec) 12X per week $_____ (3X 5:30a-10a, 3X 10a-3p, 3X 3p-7p, 3X 7p-mid)

18X per week $_____ (4X 5:30a-10a, 5X 10a-3p, 5X 3p-7p, 4X 7p-mid)

24X per week $_____ (6X 5:30a-10a, 6X 10a-3p, 6X 3p-7p, 6X 7p-mid)

*Cost per week based on weekends Friday–Sunday 10A–10P

(:60 sec) 12X per week $_____ (4X 10a-3p, 4X 3p-7p, 4X 7p-10p)

18X per week $_____ (6X 10a-3p, 6X 3p-7p, 6X 7p-10p)

24X per week $_____ (8X 10a-3p, 8X 3p-7p, 8X 7p-10p)

*Sponsorships Available (based on :60 second spots)

Type of Sponsorship	Times per Week	Price per Week	Audience
News Billboards are/are not included	2X (T, Th) 3X (M, W, F) 5X (M-F)	$_____ $_____ $_____	_____ (age) _____ (sex)
Weather Billboards are/are not included	2X (T, Th) 3X (M, W, F) 5X (M-F)	$_____ $_____ $_____	_____ (age) _____ (sex)
Sports Billboards are/are not included	2X (T, Th) 3X (M, W, F) 5X (M-F)	$_____ $_____ $_____	_____ (age) _____ (sex)
Air Traffic Billboards are/are not included	2X (T, Th) 3X (M, W, F) 5X (M-F)	$_____ $_____ $_____	_____ (age) _____ (sex)

Sample General Weekday Schedules

12X	M	T	W	Th	F
5:30-10A	X		X		X
10-3P		X	X	X	
3-7P	X		X		X
7-10P		X	X	X	

Cost $_____

18X	M	T	W	Th	F
5:30-10A	X		X	X	X
10-3P	X	X	X	X	X
3-7P	X	X	X	X	X
7-10P	X	X	X	X	

Cost $_____

24X	M	T	W	Th	F
5:30-10A	XX	X	X	X	X
10-3P	X	X	XX	X	X
3-7P	X	XX	X	X	X
7-10P	X	X	X	XX	X

Cost $_____

Sample Schedules for Early-Mid Week Business

12X	M	T	W
5:30-10A	X	X	X
10-3P	XX	X	X
3-7P	X	XX	X
7-10P	X	X	

Cost $_____

18X	M	T	W
5:30-10A	XX	X	XX
10-3P	XX	XX	XX
3-7P	XX	X	
7-10P	XX	XX	

Cost $_____

24X	M	T	W
5:30-10A	XXX	XX	XX
10-3P	XX	XXX	XX
3-7P	XXX	XX	
7-10P	XX	XXX	

Cost $_____

Sample Schedules for Late Week and Weekend Business

12X	M	T	W	Th	F	Sa
5:30-10A			X	X	X	
10-3P			X	X		X
3-7P			X		X	X
7-10P			X	X		

Cost $_____

18X	M	T	W	Th	F	Sa
5:30-10A				X	X	XX
10-3P				XX	X	XX
3-7P				X	XX	XX
7-10P				X	XX	X

Cost $_____

24X	M	T	W	Th	F	Sa
5:30-10A				X	XX	XX	X
10-3P				X	X	XX	XX
3-7P				X	XX	XX	X
7-10P				X	XX	XX	X

Cost $_____

Sample Schedules for Weekend Business

12X	F	Sa	Su
5:30-10A			
10-3P		XX	XX
3-7P	XX	XX	
7-10P	XX	XX	

Cost $_____

18X	F	Sa	Su
5:30-10A			
10-3P		XXX	XXX
3-7P	XXX	XXX	
7-10P	XXX	XXX	

Cost $_____

24X	F	Sa	Su
5:30-10A			
10-3P		XXXX	XXXX
3-7P	XXXX	XXXX	
7-10P	XXXX	XXXX	

Cost $_____

If you are not open Sunday or your event ends on Saturday, move Sunday spots back into Friday and Saturday. Or feel free to ask for a 10 pm cutoff time on any schedule.

Chapter 11

Radio Production

A WELL-PRODUCED RADIO SPOT CAN INSPIRE THE IMAGINATION LIKE nothing else. Without a video aspect, the listener's mind is free to wander—to conjure up splendid and impossible scenarios to hold their interest, make them laugh, and, most of all, to pay attention! People listening to radio are usually doing something else at the same time—driving, working in the home or at the office, or exercising—so they don't necessarily hear every word in a commercial. It has to be good!

Obviously your production will need to be done at one of the stations you will be using. But once you have tried the production at a few stations and you feel comfortable with the quality of one particular station, use that production facility for as much of your work as you can.

These are the costs involved:

▶ **Production fees:** If you are using the spot only on the station that produces it, you will most likely not be charged anything.

▶ **Dubs and talent fees:** If you take that spot to another station, you will be charged for the talent (the person who does the voiceover) and a nominal amount for any copies (dubs) of the spot for the other stations.

One of the wonderful things about radio production is that you have the option of having each station you use produce its own version of the same script. This saves you talent fees and the cost of dubs. The message will be the same—but the delivery will end up being very different, unless you give instructions that will standardize the spots.

Standardizing is very important, because you want people to know they are hearing a commercial for the same businesses when they hear slightly altered versions on different stations.

To standardize the sound of the spots done on different stations:

▶ Request a female or male voice on all spots.

▶ Request the same music.

▶ Spell out the kind of energy you want put into the voice ("energetic read" or "laid-back, casual read").

This way, each audience will hear the same words and receive the same message at little or no production cost to you. While it may be more appealing to have the same exact commercial on all stations, new businesses do not always have funds to pay even for the modest cost of radio production. And in that case it is smarter to put whatever money you have into the frequency of the schedule and run a basic but informative ad. However, if you can manage the cost of having one commercial produced (including talent fee and the cost of copies to give to other stations you are using), it's a plus to have the same commercial running on all stations.

Length of Spots

Generally, you will be running a 60-second spot. This gives you plenty of time to get your business name and location in at least three times. The name and location of your business should be mentioned at least twice in a 30-second ad and three times in a 60-second ad.

Since radio production is so inexpensive and often free, you don't have to be worried about changing your ad often. You can therefore be very specific with each script and make the ad generic or dedicate it to a special sale or promotional event. If you are having a sale, give price and item (jargon for "mention specific products and prices"), a percentage off, or a specific brand being sold at a discounted price.

You will find there is little or no room in 30 seconds for cute comments, sound effects, or even for a two-voice script. Save those extras for your 60-second scripts.

One of the wonderful things about radio production is that you have the option of having each station you use produce its own version of the same script.

If you have lots of information to cover, create either one 60-second script or two 30-second commercials, splitting the information between the two and rotating both ads throughout your schedule. When rotating two or more commercials, be sure that the opening, the voice, the music, and the general feeling of the ads are the same, so your audience will hear all of the information in both ads without being distracted by differences between the two. Remember that there's nothing to keep you from rotating two or more 60-second spots in the same schedule as well.

Add some 15-second spots to your schedule to build frequency at a lower per-spot cost. Your account executive can help you cull the most important information out of your 60-second or 30-second spot to create this shorter version.

Ads Ready to Go

It may not be necessary for you to create ads from scratch. There may be other possibilities.

Franchise operators will often have access to canned radio commercials through their advertising support system. A single phone call can put a professionally produced commercial in your hands within a day or two. Usually there will be an eight- to 10-second blank space at the end of these commercials for "tagging" with your local address and phone number.

If you're in retail sales, you may find that distributors of brand name merchandise also have professionally produced radio commercials ready to go and often co-op advertising assistance is available in the form of not only commercials but also money.

Whether you have a commercial created from scratch or you're just tagging a co-op spot, always ask to hear the final product before it airs. The station(s) will be happy to play it for you over the phone or provide a cassette. Feel free to ask that the voice be more upbeat or that the music be changed to suit you. Listen to it again after the changes have been made. Give your radio rep as much lead time as possible to avoid a last minute rush on changes.

Once your commercial has been produced, ask your rep to give you the master reel or CD if you think you might use the spot again in the future. Radio stations will store the master copies, but on a rare occasion one can be misplaced. If your ad has the potential to be used again, keep it where you can find it in a hurry. Label the box with the date and title and put a copy of the typed script with it.

TIP: Request a "client copy" of all radio spots on a cassette or CD for yourself at the time of production. You should not be charged for this service and you will then have the ability to review your ads to see if you need to make any changes before using them again in the future.

30-Second Radio Copy Form

Using an 11-point font, use this eight-line sheet for a standard 30-second script. Do not use any abbreviations, numerals, or substitutions, such as "&" for "and." All words take the same amount of time to *say* no matter how you write them. So, for an accurately timed script, spell out all words. (Recreate this form on a letter-size page for the eight-line rule to work.)

1.
2.
3.
4.
5.
6.
7.
8.

Client: _____

Title of Spot: _____

Runs ____/____/____ to ____/____/____

Special instructions: _____

_____

_____

_____

_____

_____

60-Second Radio Copy Form

Use this type of sheet for a standard 60-second script.

1.

2.

3.

4.

5.

6.

7.

8.

9.

10.

11.

12.

13.

14.

15.

16.

Client: _____

Title of Spot: _____

Runs ____/____/____ to ____/____/____

Special instructions: _____

_____

_____

_____

_____

_____

Chapter 12

Television

TELEVISION IS NOT EASY TO IGNORE, WITH ITS SIGHT, SOUND, AND motion. Unlike the newspaper that you must pick up and concentrate on or the radio that you can easily tune out while you're working on something around the house, the television makes itself the center of attention by shouting, "Hey! Look at me!"

Rob Cherof, Executive Vice President and Management Director at BBDO in Atlanta (*www.bbdoatl.com*), says, "Despite all the prognostications that no one watches TV anymore, it remains the single best way to reach the most people with the most impact in the shortest amount of time. Used properly, its branding power is unmatched."

Television segments a broadcast day in two ways:

► As specific *types* of programming, such as primetime, daytime, early news, late news, sports, specials, late fringe and children's shows

► By *day parts*: Morning (5:30 A.M.-9 A.M. Monday-Friday), Daytime (9 A.M.-4 P.M. Monday-Friday), Early Fringe (4 P.M.-7 P.M. Monday-Friday), Access (7 P.M.-8 P.M. Saturday and Sunday), Primetime (8 P.M.-11 P.M. Monday-Saturday and 7 P.M.-11 P.M. on Sunday), and Late Fringe (any regularly scheduled programming after 11:30 P.M. Monday-Friday), all based on EST.

Television ratings are usually based on *estimated* ratings—the number of households or persons expected to tune in to a particular program based on the number that tuned into similar shows that aired previously.

Although there are many television stations in any given market, you have to do some investigative work to decide whether network TV or cable TV is for you.

Although there are many television stations in any given market, you have to do some investigative work to decide whether network TV or cable TV is for you.

▶ Network TV offers a variety of programming every single day. Cartoons, sports, news, soaps, game shows, talk shows, movies, and late night shows allow you to reach every conceivable demographic by carefully choosing the programs in which you want your commercials to run.

▶ Cable TV is more like radio in that each station, in its entirety, attracts a particular segment of the population. Lifetime Movies, Food Network, HGTV, ESPN, Comedy Central, Nickelodeon, TLC, etc., all reach specific audiences.

With cable:

▶ You can choose to run your commercials in specific geographic areas.

▶ You can afford greater frequency because of the lower per-spot cost.

▶ You can choose specific programming within a station without a large boost in rate.

▶ Your commercial is far less likely to be "bumped" for clients willing to pay higher rates or by political ads.

▶ Trade advertising is accepted, depending upon your product or service.

▶ Production costs are reasonable.

▶ While local networks may be sold out in a particular business quarter, cable can almost always find appropriate space for you on one or more of its many stations.

With network:

▶ Your commercial will be seen in areas outside of your business location's geographic area.

▶ The per-spot cost is higher than with cable, so you can buy fewer spots.

▶ Advertising during the most popular programs can run hundreds of dollars per spot.

▶ Your commercial is more likely to be "bumped" for clients willing to pay higher rates for your spot or for political advertising.

▶ Trade advertising is accepted, depending upon your product or service.

▶ Production costs more than with cable.

So why buy network at all?

One major reason is that cable has smaller audiences. You may reach more people with one $400 news spot on a network station than you would with eight $50 spots on cable. Even with the number of cable channels available to people these days, it still seems to be the networks that capture a lot of the attention and excitement when it comes to new programming.

Cable has stations like TVLand that runs old television shows like *I Love Lucy*, *Leave It to Beaver*, *Bewitched*, etc. and is touted as nostalgia. When people turn to TVland, they *know* they're going to get a rerun. In contrast, network reruns seem to annoy people. When they turn on a network channel hoping for a new show and get a rerun, it's a disappointment.

During the summer, when everything but news, soaps, morning shows, and late night shows is in reruns, refuse to pay the same dollar amount for specific programming. For instance, don't pay the same amount of money for a rerun of an *Oprah* show during the summer as you would pay for a new show in the winter. The rate sheets you see will reflect one cost for *Oprah*. It's up to you to let your television rep know that *you* know that it's rerun season. It seems like a no-brainer, but if you don't mention it, they won't either.

What Do I Buy?

Frequency in television advertising is critical, as it is in all forms of advertising. The greatest commercial is worthless if no one sees it. Audiences are bombarded with 20-30 commercials for every hour of programming. To optimize your television buy, choose network programs and cable stations that closely target your audience. If you can afford a mix, cable will add frequency to your network television schedules at a lower cost while letting you target key demographics with its specialized station programming. After choosing the best programs for your business, you have to give people a chance to see and hear your message. There are three kinds of schedules you can run:

To optimize your television buy, choose network programs and cable stations that closely target your audience.

▶ Flight schedules (also known as "tactical" advertising): two to eight consecutive weeks of high-frequency advertising, whenever needed throughout the year.

- ▶ Maintenance schedules (also known as "strategic" advertising): long-term, low-frequency schedules.
- ▶ Pulsing: a schedule of one week on, one week off or two weeks on and two weeks off.

Flight schedules are often used by seasonal advertisers or for special sales, etc. For example, I work with an amusement park that is open during the months of June, July, and August (depending on the weather). The entire budget for this park is placed during these three months, but we still have to watch the weather to determine when to run commercials. If it's raining and cold in June, we run nothing until July. So some years we run a a Memorial Day special and sometimes we don't get anything started until Father's Day. If you're having a sale or a special event or if your product is seasonal, you will be dealing in tactical advertising.

Maintenance schedules are used for products or services with no seasonal aspect or for high-ticket, infrequently purchased products like large appliances and vehicles. For example, I work with a lighting center that needs business all year long. At the beginning of each year, we lay out a maintenance plan that will run consistently all year long. It serves as a base to keep the public reminded of the business name and locations, and to alert them to various discounts on particular lines of light fixtures throughout the year. Then, during the year we add in some short flight schedules to highlight sales.

A popular way to make the most of a low-frequency, maintenance television schedule (available for the most part on network TV) is to purchase a sponsorship.

A popular way to make the most of a low-frequency, maintenance television schedule (available for the most part on network TV) is to purchase a *sponsorship*. You purchase the right to have your business credited with bringing the news, sports, weather, traffic reports, etc., to the viewers. This sponsoring is done with identifying *billboards or sponsor IDs*. Billboards announce, "This edition of the news is brought to you by the XYZ Paint Company." Along with the identifying billboard the paint company receives a 30-second spot within close proximity to the actual report.

Sponsorships are usually purchased on long-term contracts, meaning at least 13 weeks and often 26 or 52 weeks. You can usually purchase a sponsorship for two to five days per week, depending on your budget. Week in and week out, your company is credited with your chosen report(s) and the audience gets used to hearing your name. Plus sponsorships are attached to new programming, not reruns, giving you a better audience.

You can also choose a specific type of programming that all networks carry at the same time, such as the six o'clock or 11 o'clock news and buy the same slot on all of the affiliates in your market on the same day. This is called *roadblocking*, ensuring that you catch just about everyone watching television at that particular time. It's especially effective for news and soap opera programming, where there are no reruns and large, loyal audiences.

Use Specialized Programming

All day long cable's Food Network is the perfect vehicle for reaching people interested in cooking. I produced a special commercial for a client of mine who owns two lighting fixture centers. We targeted kitchen lighting fixtures. I even had him wear a chef's apron and filmed the commercial in a kitchen setting. Even though my client carries many other types of light fixtures, we reached a specific "kitchen" audience by customizing the spot and running it only on the Food Network. We did the same thing for a specific cable *show*. We filmed the outdoor lighting fixtures in my client's showroom and wrote a commercial using the words "Improve the curb appeal of your home...."—and we ran the spot *only* on the show *Curb Appeal*. Again, we customized a commercial to grab the attention of people interested in fixing up the outside of their homes. You can customize your commercial to run successfully on any specific cable station, like Food Network, or just one show, like *Curb Appeal*.

Kitchen lighting commercial

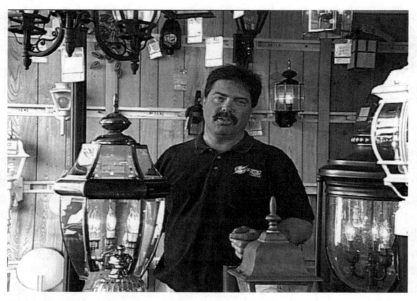

Outdoor lighting fixtures commercial
Photos courtesy of Solvay Lighting Centers in Solvay, NY and Fayetteville, NY

It's a no-brainer for a retail golf equipment store to run ads within specialty programs, such as televised golf tournaments. This guarantees the right audience and eliminates the worry about saturating the market with high frequency when your budget is small. What could be better than a captive audience with an interest in your product?

Always ask your television reps to supply you with a list of programming so you can see exactly what they have to offer. But be careful. Just because cable's Oxygen Channel, for instance, is geared toward women, you need to keep in mind that it appeals to women of *different ages* on different days and at different times of the day. Don't buy a bunch of commercials that will run willy-nilly through the week on that channel because you want to reach women 45+ and it's a movie channel. It's great for reaching those women *sometimes*, but if you don't specify where you want your spots to run you may end up running in *Xena: Warrior Princess*—which is not going to reach your desired audience.

When to increase your television schedules:

▶ You begin to carry a new, popular brand.

▶ You open a new location or move your one location.

▶ You change store policies, such as in-store financing, delivery, or mail order service.

▶ You're holding a large sale or a special event.

▶ Anytime you begin to use a new station.

Each station, whether cable or network, will be able to supply you with a coverage map to show you exactly what areas it covers. By looking at a coverage map like the one below, you can determine if a given television station will be beneficial for your location(s).

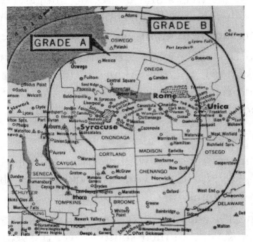

Figure 12-1. A TV coverage map

As you see, it's basically the same kind of map as was shown in the radio section of this book.

Contracts

Your television media sales reps will give you rates for first quarter, second quarter, third quarter, and forth quarter. First quarter has the lowest rates of the year and is the best time to negotiate long-term contracts—business is down and sales managers are hungry for long term contracts to bolster sagging budgets. The rates for each program are like the stickers on new cars: use them as a starting point and always ask for a break. You can expect to receive a 5-percent discount for a 26-week contract and a 10-percent discount on a 52-week contract. If you commit to running a very low number of commercials (three or four per week) at one of these discount levels, the same discount may or may not also apply to any additional schedules you run during the life of the contract.

Both network and cable stations will have special deals for you to consider during January of each year, some with names like "Upfront Package" or "Grabber" or some other cutesy name. These packages, which usually need to be finalized by the end of January, can be used to lower the per-spot-cost of what you will pay all year long.

On network stations:

▶ You will commit to a specific number of commercials that you will run during the next 52 weeks and a specific budget. You do not have to know exactly when you will run those spots at the time you sign up, as long as you do run them all in the agreed-upon time.

▶ You will need to decide what programs you want to include in your schedule, looking for the ones that will target your desired audience. You have to do this so that a per-spot cost can be determined and the number of spots you can afford can be decided.

On cable stations:

▶ You can commit to run spots within certain stations (Lifetime, Comedy Central, TLC, ESPN, etc.) or you can pick specific shows, like I did for the client I had running on *Curb Appeal*.

▶ Cable also offers a package that consists of hundreds of commercials that will run on several of their stations over the year. The commercials show up now and then—you can't really decide how many will run in the morning or in the afternoon or evening. You pay your money and take your chances.

▶ Here again, on cable you can decide to include certain geographic areas and eliminate all others, which can keep the cost of each spot as low as an incredible $4 to $8 each.

Lower rates can also apply to third quarter. Second and fourth quarters are where your rates will be highest and where bidding sometimes occurs when spots go to those willing to pay the most money for them. Your spots may be "bumped" to other areas to make room for higher-paying clients. Not fair, but it's the way it is. Your rep should call and alert you to these changes and discuss with you where your spots are expected to fall. You have the option to just cancel them if you want to.

You may also find that your schedule is violated by program changes. Advertisers whose schedules are interrupted by cancellation of unpopular new shows, replacement of regular shows with "specials," or the moving of a show to a new day or time slot are taken care of in a variety of ways:

▶ Make-good spots can be given in comparable time slots.

▶ The advertiser's spots can follow the show to the new time.

▶ The schedule is canceled and a credit or rebate is given.

All advertising units are perishable commodities. Once an empty space has gone by, it cannot be recaptured for sale at another time. While some stations or publications will come down in price at the last minute to sell vulnerable inventory, others will let it go unsold to protect the integrity of the normal rates and also to avoid "backlash buying" from advertisers who then won't go back to paying a higher rate. Actually, none of them try to hit a 100 percent sold-out position. They may need the space for make-good spots, trade, last-minute schedules, or other situations requiring the use of that extra inventory.

TV is among the most difficult media for novices to negotiate.

▶ If your budget is small, ad agencies and media buying firms won't have an interest in helping you because they cannot earn a reasonable profit for the time spent invested. (Low-budget media schedules are often just as time-consuming to place as high-budget schedules.)

▶ Small business owners with a small budget might start by meeting with a few of the local TV sales reps and asking them for names of local freelance media buyers who might be willing to work with a small budget.

▶ Ask for proposed schedules from at least two media buyers to compare rates.

▶ Ask TV sales reps for schedule proposals.

▶ With very small budgets, it is sometimes wiser to spend all of your money with one station to build frequency.

In every market there are a few advertisers who negotiate "remnant rates" with an agreeable television station. This must be a client whose product or service has wide appeal and can find an audience at any time, on any day. The contract states that the reps will contact the advertiser at the last minute on a daily or weekly basis and advise him or her of unsold space. The advertiser agrees to purchase a portion of the unsold space for a specified dollar amount. The contract can indicate a maximum number of commercials per week or per month that the advertiser agrees to buy without notification. Rates are very low for remnant advertising, but it is not a wise choice for business owners looking for a specific demographic. You will lose too many spots to audiences that will not be interested in your product or service. This is wasting your money, no matter how you look at it. Whatever type of schedule you're going for, don't be afraid to let your reps know you have other stations to choose from and that you are looking around for the best deal.

At an average 12 messages per half hour during a Monday-Friday week, 456 commercials run during an average 5 A.M.-midnight day. How many commercials can you afford to run in one day? It has to be enough to be seen and heard when surrounded by those hundreds of other commercials. Along the same line of thought, approximately 2,280 commercials will run during an average Monday-Friday, 5 A.M.-midnight week. Can you compete in all of that?

Weekends can have more openings yet. Now, not every commercial opening has to be filled by television account executives. Television programs, for instance, arrive at the stations with national commercials already inserted into the breaks and some openings are left to be filled with local clients. However, you must consider every commercial when thinking about how many of your own commercials you should run to get your message through to your audience.

Trade Advertising

Trade is a great way to advertise when cash is in short supply. Television stations have the need for many products and services for themselves. You should let your reps know up front if you are interested in these trade opportunities when they come along. You can trade gift certificates for restaurants, hotels, tickets to concerts, movies and plays, limousine service, auto repair, business machines, office furniture, and cleaning services. Vehicles for their news departments, cars for management and the care of those vehicles, and products for on-air promotions are only a fraction of items and services a station will trade for advertising.

Always think of your trade as having the same value as cash. Remember to use your highest retail price or hourly rate when figuring out a trade agreement—the stations will not be figuring in a cut rate for the cost of their airtime. And put an end date on all trade contracts so it is clear when your responsibilities are over.

Most stations will work with a 50/50 contact, which means you pay for your advertising with half cash and half trade. Be aware that the trade portion of your ads will be vulnerable to being bumped if the station needs the space for paying customers. One way to give your trade spots a better shot

TIP: Does your business require you to enter customer homes for estimates, cleaning, or installations? Be aware of what program is on the television when you are there. Keep a list.

TIP: Request a minimum of 15 minutes separation time between your television spots and those being run by your competitors.

at not getting bumped is to ask your rep to list the same rate for your trade spots on the contract as he or she lists for the paid spots. Most times they will show a dollar amount on the contract for your cash spots and then assign $0 for the trade spots. This absence of rate makes them vulnerable to be bumped. If they retain the *same value on paper*—the same dollar amount as the cash spots—they will not be the first trade spots to pop up in the computer for taking a ride on the bump-mobile.

Worksheet

Circle your predetermined demographic choices from Groups A and B on the Television Worksheet. Then have your account executives complete and return them to you. Keep *all* of your Network Television Worksheets, but keep only those Cable TV Worksheets that have opportunities for you to reach your target audience. (For example, if you're trying to reach women 45+ you'll want to keep the worksheet for Lifetime, but not Comedy Central.)

Your salespeople are instructed to list only programs that match your specific demographics. Use a separate worksheet for each cable station, just as you would for each of the network stations.

Once these worksheets are completed, you will have a list of programs watched by your potential customers on both local network and cable stations and you will know at a glance what a 30-second spot in each show costs.

TELEVISION WORKSHEET
Have Your Reps Fill Out and Return This Sheet

Note to Account Executive: Include only programs geared to demographics noted below:

Station _____ Network _____ Cable _____

Dial Position _____

Rep's Name _____

Phone # _____ E-mail _____

Account: _____

Business Owner: Circle choices from groups A and B that correspond with those you chose in Define Your Market (Chapter 5).

Group A (age)	Group B (gender)
18-34	Female
18-49	Male
25-54	Adults (both male and female)
45+	

Weekdays

Time Period	Program	Price Per :30	Per :10/:15

Weekends

Time Period	Program	Price Per :30	Per :10/:15

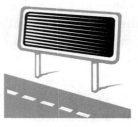

Chapter 13

Television Production

E VERYONE YOU WORK WITH ON YOUR ADS, FROM BEGINNING TO END, must all be on the same page for things to make sense when the process is concluded. Julie H. Wilson, President and CEO of Reasons Group, Inc. in Fort Worth, TX (*www.reasonsgroup.com*), says:

Work from a plan. Develop your own graphic standards and tonality of message, and insist that everyone who helps you with advertising adhere to those standards ... both inside and outside your company. Actually creating ads should be one of the last steps you take. Too often, do-it-yourselfers think up a clever headline or cute visual and jump right into production. The result by year-end is a mess of mixed messages, no brand identity, and unrelated albeit clever ideas that haven't positioned you in the minds of your consumer. Do not sacrifice strategy for creativity.

Once you have the perfect message crafted, you need to find the right people to produce your television commercial. First, inquire about production costs at each of the stations you've decided to use. If you'll be using some cable TV, you will probably find the most favorable production rates there.

Your television sales rep will assist you in writing the copy and can make suggestions for music and a voice. Since you will most likely be using a 30-second TV spot, ask whoever voices it to also voice a 60-second version (no video—just the voice). You'll pay a talent fee to move it from the station, but you can use it for radio advertising, tying it directly to your TV ad for continuity. Your television rep will help you modify the script(s) for the longer length.

There are decisions to make. What voice or voices will you use? Will the spot be produced with or without music?

You can produce:

- ▶ A generic 30-second spot.
- ▶ A 30-second spot dedicated to a sale or special event.
- ▶ A "donut" (produce the beginning and end of the spot, leaving a "hole" in the middle that can be changed).
- ▶ A generic 30-second spot with the last 10 seconds left blank (for "tagging" or changing).
- ▶ A 10- or 15-second spot to accompany any of the above. These add frequency to your schedule while keeping the cost down. Don't run these short spots alone. They have more impact when used in combination with :30s.

The third choice above is convenient and cost-effective since you can change the copy in the donut to suit different purposes.

The fourth choice listed above is also a good way to keep costs down over time. You can keep your commercial fresh and current by leaving the last 10 seconds of the spot blank so that you can change out information as needed for sales and promotions. If you've developed several sales or promotions that you will continue to run on an annual basis, you have the ability to produce one ad for each specific sale as well as a basic generic ad that you can use for longer than one year.

Always have the production person save the original generic spot in its entirety so you can go back to it again without generating additional production cost. The costs involved vary depending on how many stations you will air the commercial on.

Costs involved:

- ▶ **Production fees:** You will be charged an hourly rate for shooting on location and for editing the commercial in the studio. Now and then a promotion comes along that includes free production for a spot that will run within a station's special event.
- ▶ **Dubs and talent fees:** If you take your commercial to another station,

There are decisions to make. What voice or voices will you use? Will the spot be produced with or without music?

96

you will be charged for the talent (the person who does the voiceover) and a nominal amount for any dubs (copies) of the spot for the other stations.

I asked Mike Verostek, Production Supervisor, and Len DeLucia, Producer/Director, both of Time Warner Cable in Syracuse, NY, some questions about production in general. Here's what they had to say:

1. What requests or questions do you receive about production that make you shiver?

- ▶ I want something new, different, and unique.
- ▶ Be creative with it.
- ▶ Just put something together; I'll know what I want after I see it.
- ▶ Do you shoot on film?
- ▶ Can you shoot this in one hour?
- ▶ If I bring in my home footage, can you use it with yours?

2. What things should an advertiser have with him or her at the time of production?

- ▶ Any agreed-upon talent, extras, props, product for the shoot. Talent should be on time.
- ▶ If we're shooting vehicles, they need to be clean.
- ▶ If we're shooting food, be ready to prepare items that will probably have to be thrown away when we're through with them.
- ▶ A revised script, if there were any last-minute changes made. Include any extra shot or change in ad copy.

3. What things should an advertiser send in advance of production to save time?

- ▶ Logos.
- ▶ If co-op is involved, copy from the manufacturer detailing requirements.
- ▶ Key points about his or her business that should be included in the copy, or a complete script if possible.

4. Can you list the top 10 mistakes clients make when they come in for production?

- ▶ Wanting too much information in their commercial.

▶ Identifying their strengths against the competition, then failing to use it. We have a client who constantly insists he has better prices than the guy up the street who sells a similar product, but he won't put price points in his ads.

▶ Getting tired of an idea too quickly. Just because you notice your commercial every time it comes on doesn't mean everyone else does as well. If the viewer doesn't need a dining room table, they don't care about what your spot looks like. But the minute they decide they want one, they'll pay attention.

▶ Not identifying or focusing on the core business that they want to sell.

▶ Producing a warm and fuzzy image spot that over time may build their business, when what they really want is to sell the one hundred recliners in their warehouse by the end of the month.

▶ Including too many different aspects about their business in the ad.

▶ Using family members as spokespeople because they look "cute."

▶ Trying to incorporate video effects that they see in the movies.

▶ Wanting to use current copyrighted songs as music bed for their ads.

▶ Not allowing ample turnaround time from concept to completion.

5. What is your opinion of business owners appearing in their own commercials?

▶ They all have varying on-camera skill levels and visual appeal. I need to assess their skill after a face-to-face meeting, then make a decision.

▶ If they believe in their product and message, and can speak effectively, it works great. People walk into a store and see a face they can immediately relate to. If the product and message get lost, it doesn't matter who delivers the line.

6. What are some money-saving tips that new advertisers should know about production?

▶ Factory footage: We can't shoot a car or couch or carpet any better than the factory.

▶ Produce a donut—a spot that can be shot once and edited over and over to highlight monthly specials without the need for reshooting and rescripting.

▶ Know in advance what you're going to be selling. If recliners are going on sale next month, we can shoot specific footage while we're on location. If we have to make a second trip to shoot three chairs, it costs to send a crew out again.

► Think ahead. An advertiser who has a monthly sale "this Friday, Saturday, and Sunday only" doesn't need the dates in the commercial's voiceover or even in the commercial itself. Being able to reuse a voiceover and graphics from a previous spot makes production quicker and less expensive.

► Car dealerships should know in advance where all of the cars they want in the spot are parked. It can go from a two-hour shoot to a four-hour shoot without being organized.

Save money now and later. Your sales rep can give you suggestions on production choices. For instance, it's less expensive to produce a basic commercial using 8-by-10-inch photos than for a camera crew to come to your location to shoot an hour of footage and then go back to the studio for editing.

If you decide to have a camera crew come to your business location, have them save *all* of the raw footage they shoot that day. Remember that out of the hour or two they spend at your place, they will use only 20-30 seconds in your spot. You can go back and use different portions of the original footage later for new spots without having to pay the camera crew to come back.

It is not acceptable to use your own personal equipment to shoot the video. There are minimum standards established by the FCC that the stations must meet regarding the quality of the commercials they run, and you certainly don't want a slick national spot to run right before your amateurish ad.

Some of the items that make television production more costly:

► On-location shoots

► Special effects or animation

► Elaborate sets

► Professional casting and celebrity talent fees

► Extensive editing

► Writing and producing original music

Go to the production session. It's an interesting process to watch and it will give you the chance for input while the work is in progress. It will take less time and cost less than it would to have to go back to make changes after the first production in finished. If you're right there, you can suggest changes in the visuals, the music, or the voice. Be satisfied with the final product!

If you are going to be running your commercials on only one station, you will not have to pay a talent fee to have your spot produced (unless you're bringing in special talent). But if you want to run the spot on another station, you *will* have to pay a talent fee to the person who voices your spot, as well as for each dub of the spot. If your talent is a highly visible personality, such as the station's meteorologist or sportscaster, you may not be able to take that commercial to another station at all. Using a well-known or famous person in your ad can have its own special kind of problems.

I made that very mistake years ago when I developed a PSA campaign for a United Way agency. I contacted local celebrities, radio and television personalities, politicians, and community leaders to record congratulatory messages for the agency's 100th anniversary. One of the on-air personalities was fired, another went to work for another station, and one of the politicians was voted out of office, so all of those spots were unusable after time, money, and effort had been expended. Luckily we had enough people left intact to carry on the campaign, but what a hassle!

Come to production prepared! Since you're being charged by the hour, you'll save money if you have finalized the copy and decided on the talent and music ahead of time. If you are using still photos, you should send them to the station several days in advance, along with a clean copy of your logo, address, phone number, URL, and business hours. If you are shooting at your location, decide ahead of time what you want in the commercial. Do a dress rehearsal if you have to in order to waste as little time as possible at the actual event. Props should be discussed, located, and brought to the studio or your location at least two days ahead to avoid last-minute delays that could prolong or ruin your schedule.

Leave your Uncle Barney at home! So your kids are cute, your brother-in-law is an aspiring actor and wants a shot at being discovered, your sister thinks she can sing, and your dog is almost a person. Leave them at home. It's hard to find a less professional-looking and -sounding commercial than one in which a client's family member or beloved pet, or even the client himself or herself appears. It happens all the time and it's even a great sales tool: account execs know that a client will run an ad more often if a member of his or her family is in the commercial. It's an ego thing. Don't do it!

Yes, I know: I did what I just told you not to do! In the previous chapter, I showed you photos of one of my clients appearing in his own commercials. This is one of the few exceptions—and, by the way, this is only the second time I have done this in the 20 years my agency has been around.

Using a well-known or famous person in your ad can have its own special kind of problems.

This particular client has sort of a macho, tousled, guy thing going on and he comes across as very personable and "real." There are precious few exceptions (such as the late Dave Thomas of Wendy's) where the owner of a business should be involved. In general, they *and their families* should stay away from the camera. We don't all look kindly, humorous, cuddly, or even nice—and we're not good judges of how we appear or sound to others. Clearly, we don't want to do anything to impede the production of a crisp, concise, product- or service-enhancing ad.

A professional's appearance and voice will not distract in any way from the intent or message of the commercial. If you have a wiggling child reciting memorized lines in a monotone and staring at the camera like a deer caught in headlights, you have no chance of having your message received. Similarly, your dog in a fisherman's hat or sitting in a recliner with a cigar sticking out of his mouth and his eyes darting from side to side like he needs to go out will totally thwart your commercial message. Even if you have to sneak out of the house, leave them all at home!

Give the script to your radio or television account executive. He or she will recommend an experienced voice and/or personality to provide you with a commercial that will shine the spotlight on your business, product, service, sale, or special event.

Consent and release. Whenever you produce a television commercial or a promotional video or develop any print or outdoor ad using the image or name of any people, whether you pay them or not, get each and every one of them to sign a consent and release form. (Parents or guardians must sign for underage children and the owners of any animals you use must also sign for their beasts.) Even if it's your best friend, your business partner, or a member of your own family, it's the smart thing to do. Unfortunately, business partners, friends, and families sometimes split up or have major disagreements. If that happens and your print ad, direct mail piece, outdoor billboard, or commercial includes the name, the image, or the voice of the former partner, friend, or relative, you can be forced to stop using that spot, ad, or design and incur the expense of producing a new one.

If you are filming in a restaurant, a bar, a store, or the street, plant the people who will be in the ad and have them sign forms well ahead of the shoot. The area should be secured so that no one else wanders into the camera range. If they do, you must obtain their signature on a consent and release form immediately. This applies to strangers as well as people you know and love. Some people choose to hang a sign in clear view alerting

TIP: Request a "client copy" of all television spots on a VHS or DVD for yourself at the time of production. You should be charged only a minimal fee or nothing at all for this service. You will then have the ability to review your ads anytime you wish to see if anything needs to be changed (like price or percentage discounts, dates, etc.) before you can use the spots again in the future.

people who walk in or through the designated area during the shoot so they can choose to avoid the camera if they wish. I still prefer to get signatures.

Keep all of your signed consent forms in a file. It's not unusual for a spot or ad to be used for months or even years unless a specific end date is written into the agreement, so don't throw the signed consent forms away! Keep them as long as you can use the material.

Chapter 14

Whatcha Gonna Say? Radio and Television

O K, YOU'RE READY TO ADVERTISE. YOU'VE PEGGED YOUR AUDIENCE and you know what radio and television stations you're going to use to reach them. Now, what are you going to say in your ads that will make your audience sit up look, listen, and then react?

"Comfort advertising" isn't going to work for you. *Comfort ads* are made up of messages that contain the basics, like your business name, address, hours, and precious little more. They're comfortable because they represent your business, they don't annoy anyone, they don't break any laws, and they're "safe." *Yawn!*

Your message, or lack of it, will be the final factor in whether people will get off of the couch and go to the phone or get into the car and actually visit your location.

If you've just opened the 23rd shoe store in town, you must know (from the branding chapter) why customers would do better coming to your shoe store than to any of the other 22.

Go back to that nugget of how your store is different (better) than the others and start with that premise. Create your ad around the branding effort you have decided will work for you. Are your prices better? Is the quality of your product superior? Are your hours and location more convenient? Do you carry odd or difficult-to-find sizes? Are your shoes all imported or are they all American-made? Designer? Knockoffs? What? Because if you don't give your potential customers a reason to bypass the other stores to get to yours, they won't.

BBDO's Rob Cherof advises,

> Great creative comes from great insights about your consumer. But you've got to look deep to find a real insight. Not just the obvious information. Anyone can do that. You need to know what keeps them up at night. What gets them excited? What is so strong that they will change their habits as a result?

If you're lucky, you may have been blessed with one or two very clever radio and television account executives who can help you write such a script. Many such people end up working for ad agencies down the road, so don't sell them short when it comes to creative ability. You can have more than one of your radio reps write scripts and produce demos for you to choose from. Television reps can't always make demos for you because of the costs. But they can give you a pretty good idea what your spot will look and sound like with a script and graphics.

Your advertising message is one of the most important segments of a successful ad. I cannot emphasize that enough. You can choose the right station, program, publication, or outdoor venue, but if your message does not capture the attention of the audience, if it is not clear and motivating, you're still wasting your money.

Tom Matzell, of MRW Communications, says,

> When you do start talking to them, be sure to tell them what they want to hear, not what you want to say. In this "What have you done for me lately?"world, do they really care that you've been in business since 19-whatever? That you are the "largest around" or "family-owned"? Give them messaging that makes them feel good, important, and valued as your customer. And by all means double that feeling when they actually walk in or buy something.

Image and Motivational Messages

Many things must be considered when you get ready to craft an advertising message. Is your business well known or brand new? Do you sell infrequently purchased high-ticket items, like major appliances, mattresses, or automobiles, or products that people stop and pick up frequently, such as groceries or dry cleaning? Perhaps you're in between those two examples of frequency and sell shoes, clothing, flowers, books, dining or entertaining experiences, massage, or hair and nail design. Or maybe you're seasonal and are open for business for only part of a year. Do you have to promote sales? Or do you need ads that will interest your customers in general on an ongoing, year-round basis?

An *image commercial* contains generic information about a business, product, or service. It's a commercial you can use as long as the information remains relevant and there are no date-specific sales or special events in the ad and no special reason for the audience to respond in a timely fashion. An image commercial gives an overall picture and perception of your business, mentions a variety of products or services available, and lists your location(s) and phone number(s) and perhaps your business hours. The audience is being told what you do or what you have there that might interest them today, tomorrow, or next year. If you're not careful, generic ads can topple over into the (yawn!) comfort zone. BBDO's Cherof advises, "If your message isn't strong and focused, it will never be heard."

The *motivational ad* provides time-sensitive information on sales, grand openings, special events, clearances, liquidation sales, etc. It is meant to create a sense of urgency in the minds of your customers, to coax them into action.

In truth, all commercials should be motivational. No one purposefully crafts a message that will turn customers away; some are just more motivational than others. So image pieces are indeed meant to interest the consumer; it's just that the motivational pieces present compelling reasons to see, visit, purchase, or order now rather than later.

An image commercial contains generic information about a business, product, or service. It's a commercial you can use as long as the information remains relevant and there are no date-specific sales or special events in the ad.

Radio

Some people like to use more than one voice in an ad. You do this more often in a 60-second ad than in a 30-second ad. Roger Hurni, Creative Director/Partner of Off Madison Ave in Tempe, Arizona (*www.offmadison-ave.com*), says:

> Radio is one of the most difficult mediums in advertising. A creative person simply has fewer tools to work with. There are no moving pictures, no photography, no illustrations, and nothing to read or refer back to. But when done properly, it can be one of the most cost-effective and results-producing advertising mediums available.
>
> In order to create great radio, you need to understand messaging. Too many radio commercials invoke a one-way communication model. They push

a message onto their audience, telling them all the facts that the advertiser feels are important. It is better to look at communication as a two-way street. You have something to say and your audience has something they want to hear. Give your customers what they want first. Try and understand what their pain points are. Your audience has to feel you understand them or the situation they're in. Be entertaining or thoughtful, make them laugh or cry. The important thing to do is connect with them emotionally.

So how do you connect with your audience and capture their attention? You have to make a point. One of the best ways to do that is to create a scenario that is so unrealistic people can see the absurdity in it. For examples, just look to any stand-up comic. They employ this kind of attention-getting technique all the time to make a point. You want great radio? Capture your audience's attention and they will hang onto your every word.

Here is an example of a radio commercial provided to us by Roger Hurni for his client, *The Arizona Republic*. The spot is called "News Family."

Dad: Okay everybody, gather around. Here are the news assignments for this week. Billy, you're covering tonight's D-Backs game, the crossword puzzle, and Thursday's school board meeting.

Billy: (Whining) Aw, Dad. I hate school board meetings.

Dad: No whining, Billy. Or I'll put you on obituaries. Sally?

Sally: Yeah, dad?

Dad: You're on classifieds. There's a guy in Glendale who wants to sell his '85 Corolla, a family in Chandler who lost their Shitzu, a refurbished copy machine for sale in Mesa, and about 150 drug stores in Phoenix that need pharmacists. Got it?

Sally: Um . . . .

Dad: (Cuts her off) Margaret?

Margaret: Yes, dear?

Dad: I was hoping you could pull together this weekend's entertainment guide.

Margaret: No problem, hon.

Dad: And I really need you on Middle Eastern policy.

Margaret: (Annoyed) Are you kidding? I just got back from the Middle East. Do you know how long that flight is?

Dad: (Angry) Well, what do you expect me to do, Margaret? Baby corn is on special and it's not gonna sell itself!!

Announcer: How do you find out what's going on? Subscribe *today* to *The Arizona Republic* and you'll get a three-month subscription for the price of two. Call (602) 444-4444. *The Arizona Republic.* Call *now* to take advantage of this three-for-two offer. (602) 444-4444. Offer good for new subscribers only.

Robert Shaw West, Chairman/CEO of The Republik, tells us:

More important than advertising itself is the need to be smart. Consumers are a pretty smart bunch. They've seen and heard it all. They are bombarded with so much information that they've become desensitized to the whole thing. So how do you engage them? By doing ads that praise their intelligence. Advertising that makes them think, laugh, relate. Advertising that reaches out and engages consumers in a way they will never forget. Advertising that makes your brand stand out above all others who choose to be less smart.

West gives this example, called "Perfect Radio":

Music: Needle Drop

Announcer: I'm here with —

Glenn: Lower.

Announcer: (*Very deep voice*) I'm here with —

Glenn: A tad higher.

Announcer: (*Higher voice*) I'm here with Quality Control Supervisor Glenn Johnson —

Glenn: Johnston — ton.

Announcer: Glenn John-ston of Re-New Anal Retentive Construction Services—what?

Glenn: Your tie has a stain on it.

Announcer: This is radio. Nobody can see my tie.

Glenn: I can. Take it off.

Announcer:(*Annoyed*) All right. Mr. John-ston and his crew of skilled crafsmen install –

Glenn: Crafts-men. It has a "t" in it like John-ston.

> **Announcer:** (*Really annoyed*) Mr. John-ston and his crew of skilled crafts—men install vinyl siding, doors, windows and roofs with obsessive compulsive perfectionism—What now?
>
> **Glenn:** The music sucks. Lose it.
>
> **Announcer:** If you demand flawless installation of vinyl siding, windows, doors, and roofing, who do you call?
>
> **Glenn:** It's "Whom do you call?"
>
> **Announcer:** Good Lord, you're annoying. For a free estimate, call Re-New Construction Services at 828-5330.
>
> **Glenn:** It's Re-New Anal Retentive Construction Services.

Unless you're prolific and have lots of time to spend laboring over a powerful and meaningful radio script, timed to exactly 30 or 60 seconds, look to your radio rep(s) to write the scripts for you.

Doing a great job putting together your commercial message can be a daunting task. Many small business owners are intimidated by the process. Unless you're prolific and have lots of time to spend laboring over a powerful and meaningful radio script, timed to exactly 30 or 60 seconds, look to your radio rep(s) to write the scripts for you.

If you are new to radio and are not sure of the talent available, have a script prepared at each of the stations you will be using and ask for a cassette from each to listen to. Choose the one you like the best and ask for one dub of the finished commercial to use on each of the other stations. The copy writing is free of charge and is done by either your sales rep or an actual copywriter employed by the station.

Don't wander. Stay focused on material that has the best chance of motivating people to come in or call. Listen to national commercials. A company promoting its shampoo will not say at the end, "And we also sell toothpaste."

Alan Webb, Senior Creative Director at Sterling-Rice Group in Durham, Colorado (*www.srg.com*), gives us some good advice:

Don't make ads about what you want to say. Make ads about what your customer wants to hear.

Simply saying that you exist and listing items you sell or services you render will not do it. Concentrate on specific information that makes it important and beneficial for people to come to your store or office instead of to one of your competitors. Make each ad a call to action! If you don't make that case, if there is no *motivation* for them to come to your location instead of a competitor, you will be one of the people who say, "I tried radio and it doesn't work."

108

If you are trying your hand at writing your own radio scripts, here are some guidelines. A 30-second script equals about eight typed lines using an 11-point font. A 60-second commercial equals approximately 16 typed lines. Replacing the word "and" with an ampersand (&) and using abbreviations such as "Blvd." or numerals for prices, like "$299.99" instead of spelling out the number "two ninety-nine, ninety-nine," will not allow you to put more words into the ad. They all take the same time to say, no matter how you write them! After the script has been timed to 30 or 60 seconds, go back and replace the numeric spellings with the actual numbers. It makes it easier for the person who will voice the ad to read it smoothly.

Also, spell out URLs and difficult words phonetically. (See the script below.) Nothing will stop a message from getting through like a mispronounced word that catches the listener's attention. The audience will hear nothing else in the ad after a mangled word. From then on, every time they hear the ad, they'll continue to listen, not for the message, but to hear the word mispronounced again. Words like "route" need to be spelled phonetically. Depending on where you live, you may want it pronounced so that it rhymes with *boot* or so that it rhymes with *scout*.

Write any instructions at the beginning of the script indicating music bed (background) selections, energy level of the read, male or female voice, where a jingle should come in, etc.

Your ad is good when it is disturbing, discomforting, funny, or awkward. When an ad gets you to rethink it, that's good. You don't want an ad that looks like something that's been done before. It should challenge you, so that it will interest the prospective target. Any ad that leaves the target indifferent is bad.

Guy Lyman, President of Guy Lyman Advertising in Dallas, Texas (*www.guylyman.com*), sent us this example of an ad that makes the audience uncomfortable. You can actually hear the ad (which is even more disturbing than reading it) at *www.guylyman.com*.

Write any instructions at the beginning of the script indicating music bed (background) selections, energy level of the read, male or female voice, where a jingle should come in, etc.

Title: WatchSoft Disk Tracy "Bad Guy" Radio 60

Male Voice: You don't know me, but I know your kid. Nice kid, kind I like best. We met on the Internet. Oh, I know, you didn't think this stuff happens to *good* kids like yours. But the fact is, even the best kids eventually come across the nasty stuff on the Internet; you know, the sex, drugs, violence … and I'm right here waiting for 'em. In fact, I just e-mailed your kid some reeeeal interesting photos.

> Another day or two, I bet I'll have your address. And there ain't nothin' you can do about it (*sinister laughing*) ....
>
> **Annoucer:** (*urgent, serious tone*) Parents, there *is* something you can do to make the Internet safe for your kids. Disk Tracy software puts a *barrier* between your kids and the things they *shouldn't see*, the people they *shouldn't meet*. Letting you *monitor* Internet activity. Call 1-888-70-WATCH to get award-winning Disk Tracy software on sale for only $34.95, satisfaction guaranteed. That's 1-888-70-WATCH. Call now!

Make the cash register ring by talking to your customers. They will give you a strategy to follow. Find the core of your product positioning, determine where you differ from your competition, and then stand on it. Evaluate everything you do as it relates to "it." If the "it" is personalized customer service, for example, then make sure that you look at every communication against that strategy and ask yourself, "Is it credible? Is it compelling? Is it different? Is it clear?"

What Do You Advertise?

Inventory-rich businesses carry priority products and goods of lesser importance. Make a list of the most critical product lines, brands, and items of high profit return. These are the items you want to look into first, because co-op dollars may be available from some of your major brands. Advertise a "hot commodity," to get people into the store. They can look around and see what else you have once they're inside.

Service-oriented businesses need to list their services in order of importance to the clients.

Service-oriented businesses need to list their services in order of importance to the clients, those you have the ability to provide in large quantity, and those with the highest rate of return per hour.

Every commercial should appeal to a specific demographic group. However, while some businesses cater only to a very specific clientele, others offer products with a more universal appeal, such as automobile dealers, music stores, grocery stores, gas stations, insurance companies, health clinics, pet shops, just to name a few. If your business can attract customers or clients from more than one specific group, you can take advantage of special deals that may come along within almost any category of advertising by varying your copy.

Let me give you an example. Every automobile dealer carries many different models, from two-seater convertible sports cars, to station wagons, to four-door family models, to 10-passenger vans, to plush, top-of-the-line, high-end luxury sedans, and now hybrids. A company like this can advertise to anyone old enough to drive! What an opportunity to take advantage of special promotions and deals from almost any station in existence! By simply writing separate scripts featuring the appropriate vehicle to attract the 18-34 crowd, the 25-54 gang, and the 50+ bunch, this business owner can target all drivers. The results can be enhanced with print ads showing pictures of the various vehicles described in the commercials. The owner can place the ads in publications that match the demographic groups of his or her radio and television schedules.

Television

Television scripts are written a little differently than radio scripts. They are generally only 30 seconds in length (or shorter) and are divided on the page into audio and video portions. They're set up so that the person editing the spot can see what is supposed to be seen and heard at the same time.

Audio	Video
SFX: Background music, as if coming from inside the house	**Dusk: Still camera:** house with interior and exterior lights on (can see flag waving and leaves on trees moving).
SFX: Clap of thunder	House lights suddenly go out. (Music stops when lights go out.)
Pause (no sound)	
SFX: Sound of generator starting	House lights come back on. (Start music when lights come back on.)
ANNOUNCER: Within 45 seconds of a power outage, this Generator System from Cutler-Hammer automatically restores electric power to your home! See what peace of mind looks like, at Solvay Lighting Centers in Solvay and in Fayetteville.	Photo of generator with AUTOMATIC GENERATOR SYSTEM written over graphic. Show Cutler-Hammer logo. Go to Solvay Lighting business info. **Flashing:** 0% financing 6 months—same as cash!

Television scripts are written a little differently than radio scripts. They are generally only 30 seconds in length (or shorter) and are divided on the page into audio and video portions.

111

Don't be afraid to be bold, funny, dramatic, or sarcastic in your ads. Some of the best ideas can be found in ad agency wastebaskets because clients can't see those tactics being employed in their own ads ... although they love them in someone else's! What sense does that make?

And be sure your commercial has made a point by the end. The generator spot increased sales for this business from two generators a month to upwards of 15! The section of the ad where the house goes dark and the music goes off leaves a silence long enough to make the audience get a little edgy, wondering if it will come back on or not. For residents of upstate New York, where weather-related blackouts have become a real nuisance, this ad struck home.

One of the benefits of television production is that you don't need to *say* everything in your television script because you have the ability to print messages on-screen along with the audio and video (such as the financing information in the generator script).

Keep the master copy of each commercial. (This is not a VHS.) Note the title of the commercial and the date of production on the box and keep a typed script of the spot attached to the box with a rubber band.

Ask your production person to make a continuous loop reel for you that contains all of your commercials so you can run them non-stop in your store. It will help customers remember your ads or make the connection between the ads and your store if they hadn't done so before.

Chapter 15

Print

PRINT IS EVERYWHERE—*DAILIES, WEEKLIES, MONTHLIES, QUARTERLIES,* inserts .... The list goes on and on. You're looking at it right now! Newspaper and specialty publication advertising have been around longer than any of us and, despite the enormous growth of radio and television advertising, print remains the leading advertising medium. Business people love print ads because they can clip them out, hang them on the wall, and 15 years later still read them and touch them—while those darn radio and television ads disappear into thin air, leaving only the hope that someone was watching or listening when they ran. And it's tough to pay an invoice for something that has disappeared into thin air.

That was the thought process of a lot of older business owners and many passed the mindset down to the next generation. Today we see the power of all forms of advertising when they are used properly and we know that print is still a wonderful form of getting our messages out.

Rob Cherof of BBDO gives us this advice: "Print is another great medium. Isn't it interesting that one of the biggest beneficiaries of the Internet has been print? Virtually every technology company uses it. And that is because it is so effective. The message is enduring. Created effectively, it is defining."

Daily newspapers offer constant market presence and are considered time-sensitive because they are generally read on the day of publication. There is a sense of immediacy about this form of advertising because every new day brings new information—and with it new advertising. Today many people get their news from television or radio simply because they don't have the time to invest in reading an entire paper. But it is one of the best places to reach the older segment of the population, people who have the time and the inclination to comb through each page.

Newspapers provide readers with more in-depth information on sales, promotions, and events, then can radio or television's vanishing 30 or 60 seconds. Print ads make it easy for consumers to do comparative shopping and to take time reading and rereading the ads that attract them. This makes newspaper advertising a wonderful partner to radio and television, allowing the "rest of the story" to be told in greater detail.

Measurement of newspapers is done by *circulation*. While the circulation figures will tell you how many papers are delivered, the information is somewhat limited in value. The circulation of a paper does not accurately portray the number of actual readers per paper. You are not able to get a handle on how many people actually read each section or how many people may read one paper delivered to a household or an office. No specific demographics are available. Think of the coverage as *potential readership* rather than actual readership. And remember that people will usually hang onto a paper long enough to receive the next copy. So dailies are discarded on a daily basis, along with your ad, while weeklies tend to stay around for the whole week.

Print ads make it easy for consumers to do comparative shopping and to take time reading and rereading the ads that attract them.

When using a daily publication, be sure to request the sections of the publication you prefer, such as sports, metro, restaurant guide, local news, etc. If you don't want your ad to show up on the obituary page, be sure and say so or it might very well end up there.

Less Expensive and More Specific

Most daily papers have a slightly less expensive neighborhood or local section delivered with the main paper or mailed separately. While the main body of a daily paper carries the same information to its entire circulation, the neighborhood sections print very specific news of individual towns and are circulated only to addresses within those towns. You can save money by advertising in just a few neighborhoods at a time with these ultra-local sections.

The weekly subscription papers in your area are wonderful for covering specific geographic locations, one at a time or all areas at once. People are likely to read a publication they have paid for, giving these papers an edge over the free shopper publications. The papers are mailed or delivered to key suburban areas—and you can choose to advertise in one or all of the available papers. Your rep will provide you with a list of circulation areas and the number of deliverable addresses within each ZIP code. You can place the same ad in all papers or alter your ad with different products or offers for different ZIP communities. The more papers you use at one time, the lower your cost will be per ad. You can feel comfortable using these subscription-based weeklies to sell higher-priced items, because they are generally mailed to higher-income households. You can sell the offer *and the benefit* of your product or service to these consumers.

The free shoppers are better for readers who are looking for bargains. A combination of an ad or insert in the free weekly shopper publication and coupons in an envelope-style mailing will work well together to target the same bargain hunters for a comparatively low cost. Sell a great offer to these buyers—forget the benefit. No high-ticket items or services.

Inserts

If you like the idea of individual direct mail pieces, but the cost of postage makes sending out large quantities prohibitive, have your flyers or coupons printed by the direct mail companies and use them as inserts in newspapers. You can control the number of flyers you print and distribute by having your flyers or coupons inserted only into papers going to the specific areas you want to target.

If your daily paper has a minimum number of insertions too large for your budget (you will be charged a fee per thousand pieces), try your weekly subscription papers or shoppers. Both will let you insert flyers or coupons into specific areas for a certain price per thousand and both will be less expensive then the daily paper, which is good news for the new business owner on a limited budget.

Call the Chamber of Commerce offices in areas you would like to penetrate and ask about the cost of inserting flyers into their monthly mailings. They will often have a program to insert hundreds of flyers into monthly mailings to members for as little as $50—great for business-to-business as well as business-to-consumer advertising. Admittedly, not everyone who receives a monthly mailing from the Chamber of Commerce, or from any other source, actually reads the whole piece each month. Sometimes secretaries or office managers pull out only what they think will be of interest to their bosses—and sometimes the mailings get buried on a messy desk. Get a list of the members, select the names or businesses you feel are outstanding prospects for your product or service, and make some phone calls a day or two ahead of the scheduled delivery to tell those prime prospects that the flyer is on its way. Then, if they're interested, they will be sure to look for it.

While this type of insertion fee may be low, you will have to pay a printer to produce your material. Your printer will be able to help you with the design and layout of your piece. Don't do it yourself—especially when you're just starting out. You want the material to look professional. Remember that everything you put into the community says something about you and your company. Trying to save on production will not be a saving in the long run if your stuff looks unprofessional.

Magazines

Magazine advertising is not always the first type of print you think of, but it can give you the ability to reach specialty markets very effectively. There are local magazines you can pick up for free on display in high-traffic locations such as grocery and drug stores, mini-marts, and gas stations. They range in subjects: real estate, restaurant guides, antique cars, and entertainment such as musical events, movies, and local theater productions, etc. If their specialty readers are of interest to you, these magazines are a great place to reach them. Pick up one or two copies of any that you can use. The numbers to call for advertising information will be printed inside. You can also check with your local Chamber of Commerce for a list of such local magazines.

Many nationally distributed magazines will have local sections you can buy.

Many nationally distributed magazines will have local sections you can buy. You may have been looking through a *Time* or *Newsweek* and stopped suddenly at a full-page ad for a business in your town. These magazines publish special sections sold on a regional basis. These ads can lend a load of credibility to your business and are useful for specialty stores, because people will travel great distances to check out a "new" supplier of a hobby. They also serve businesses with more than one location well, since their coverage areas are usually broken down into large segments of the country (Northeast, Northwest, Southeast, etc.). Fishing, specific sports, pets, cars, home decorating, parenting, health, and business are just a few types of nationally distributed magazines that sell local sections.

Layout and Production

First, let your rep(s) know what you are trying to accomplish with your ad(s). If you're having a sale, write down all of the particulars, like the name of brands or products that will be featured, and any pricing and dates that apply. Your rep(s) will take the information you provide and create a layout (design) for your approval.

When writing or approving copy for your print ads, remember to keep the main idea as simple as possible. Determine what message you need to get across and then find the shortest, clearest way to deliver it. Use phrases from daily life that everyone is familiar with to ensure instant understanding.

Determine what message you need to get across and then find the shortest, clearest way to deliver it.

No matter what kind of print you're doing, you need:

- ▶ A headline of interest
- ▶ A simple, eye-catching design
- ▶ Limited text
- ▶ A call to action

Guy Lyman, of Guy Lyman Advertising, says:

In print advertising you have only a few seconds to capture the reader's attention before she turns the page. You can stop her for a moment with a striking image—but only for a moment. Very quickly, she must be intrigued that there is some personal benefit to be gained by reading the ad. Will she have fresher breath? Will her PC run faster? Will she avoid automobile breakdowns?

There are basically two ways to accomplish this. You can creatively illustrate the benefit the product will bring to her, or you can illustrate the negative situation she will *avoid* by using the product or service.

The creator of the ad should first have a clear idea of who this person is— as though he is sitting across the desk from her. This will probably be a composite, an "ideal" prospect. With this picture in mind, he should first concentrate on getting clarity on *exactly* what he is trying to say to her. What's the promise? I inevitably find that when I am stumped trying to think up ideas, it's because I am not clear in my own mind about what I am trying to say. With this clarity, the ad creator is prepared for creative executions—ideas for how to communicate the promise in powerful ways.

When creating a heading, look for a common sentiment that will resonate with the reader (*man, I know how this guy feels!*) and then be able to solve his or her problem with your product or service. Again, team it up with the perfect picture to create something magical.

On the next page, Lyman provides us with this example of a print ad that computer-weary business owners can easily relate to.

Peter Altschuler, Vice President of Marketing and Strategy at Wordsworth & Company in Santa Monica, California (*www.wordsworthandco.com*), says:

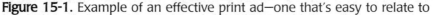

Figure 15-1. Example of an effective print ad—one that's easy to relate to

Want "great creative"? Then forget creativity … for a while, at least. Start with some market analysis—real work stuff. Like who your best buyers are and what they care about most—quality, price, service, and value. Find out what they think about your company (or product or service)—honestly, of course—and how they compare you to your close (and not so close) competition. What

118

do they think makes you different? (And pray it's a good thing.)

Now build on that. Use the perceptions the marketplace already has to develop a message you know they'll accept—one that's phrased in terms your buyers understand. So forget in-house jargon. Forget making statements that just talk about you. Customers want to know "what's in it for me?" And that means making benefits clear, beginning in the headline and (if you've got one) the visual.

Bottom line? Look at all you do from your customers' side and ask, "Why should I care?" When you can answer that—and put it in your ads, brochures, direct mail, and web sites—you'll have given your prospects a reason to respond. And that's what great creative does best.

For maximum impact, team up a great photo and a great heading! The Compaq ad on the next page was directed at teachers and appeared in an issue of *NEA Today*.

Fortify Your Ads

▶ Combine print with radio or television so that each reinforces the message of the other.

▶ Use radio or television to alert people to direct mail or newspaper ads containing "more information" or coupons redeemable at your place of business. "See Thursday's paper" or "Watch your mailbox this week for money-saving coupons."

Ask to see a proof of your ad before it runs. Check your address, phone number, dates—*everything*—to be sure it's all correct. To help your rep have time to plan your design and provide you with a proof in time to make changes, give him or her as much notice as you can—preferably a week or two before deadline. If you have a coupon in your ad, make sure it has an end date on it.

If for any reason your rep is not able to provide you with a proof and your ad runs incorrectly—e.g., if it runs on the wrong day, if the phone number is wrong—call immediately and ask for a make-good ad in the next available paper. If the next available paper is too late for your sale or special event, request a full refund or credit. One of the best reasons to see a proof before publication is to go over the ad with a fine-tooth comb to be sure there are no mistakes.

One of the best reasons to see a proof before publication is to go over the ad with a fine-tooth comb to be sure there are no mistakes.

Figure 15-2. For a great impact, team up a great photo and a great headline
Reprinted with permission from Compaq Computers

Contracts

Contracts in daily and weekly papers are commonplace, because the rate for placing one ad at a time without a contract is quite a bit higher than agreeing to place even a few ads during one year with a contract. Ad sizes are figured in *column inches*. The pages of any paper are laid out with a certain number of columns of equal width, each running straight from the top of the page to the bottom, unless broken by an advertisement. When figuring the size of an ad, you make two size determinations:

▶ How many columns *wide* do you want your ad? You can cover one column, two columns, or all of the columns on a page.

▶ How many inches *long* do you want your ad?

Let's say you want your ad to be three columns wide and five inches long. To determine the cost of that ad, you multiply three (columns) by five (inches). Your ad will be 15 column inches. If your chosen publication charges $6.00 per column inch, your ad will cost $90.00 (15 column inches X $6.00). There are price breaks for different numbers of column inches just as there are price breaks for running 24 radio spots instead of 12 in one week. The more print ads you run, the lower the cost per ad will be. Different sections of the paper and "special sections" may have different rates per column inch.

Your newspaper contract will specify a total number of column inches to be used over a 52-week period or whatever the period of time in your contract. You may commit to running only a few ads a year and you need not know exactly *when* you will use them when you sign your contract. As the year progresses, your rep will let you know how many column inches you still must run to fulfill your contract. Some papers offer both *frequency discounts* (the more often you run) and *bulk column inch discounts* (the number of ads and the size of the ads you run, combined). If you run more column inches than your contract calls for and actually reach the next price break, you may receive a rebate at the end of the year. If you don't reach your contract level, however, you may be *short-rated,* meaning you will be billed for the difference between the contract rate (which you did not meet) and the normal rate for the number of column inches you ran.

In print, size does matter. This medium, unlike any other, alerts readers to the size of your business, simply by the size of the ad you run. When your quarter-page or eighth-page ad lands next to a competitor's half- or full-page display, it dampens your attempt to project the image of your business as large and thriving. This is not the case in radio, TV, and outdoor advertising, where all businesses have the same few choices of commercial length or size.

You need not always run display ads. *Retail classified ads* are available at a much less expensive rate and appear in the classified section under specific headings. They are short, all-text ads, with no graphics.

As a new advertiser, you may be asked to pay cash in advance for your ads until you establish a credit history; this may be true with all media, but almost surely with print. When a business becomes strapped for cash, media usually feels the pinch first, by being paid late or not at all. Some papers will offer a discount for cash in advance or payment within 15 days. Once you have established a track record, you will certainly be extended 30-day credit. If, however, you fall behind at some point, you may find yourself back to a cash-in-advance status.

Your newspaper contract will specify a total number of column inches to be used over a 52-week period or whatever the period of time in your contract.

Use the KISS Theory—Keep It Simple, Stupid!

You could say, "Little Robert is displaying symptoms of a stomach ailment," or you could say, "Bobby barfed!" Use words and short phrases that are easy to understand. Keep your main message simple and understandable. Then, use it over and over, in print as well as all of your other media ads.

Keep your main message simple and understandable. Then, use it over and over, in print as well as all of your other media ads.

Pay attention to other print ads. Which ones catch your eye? Study the layout of those ads. If you are lucky enough to have a rep (whether print, radio, or television) with a fertile imagination, ask for help in coming up with something unusual, entertaining, funny, or a little off-the-wall, and then turn him or her loose. You are not bound to use whatever may result, but you might find that you want to.

Tina Karelson, Group Creative Director of Risdall Advertising in St. Paul, Minneapolis (*www.risdall.com*), says,

> The best advice I can give small business owners who are writing their own print ads is to play it straight. It's tempting to use a pun or some other cutesy device in the headline, but it's almost always a bad idea. It makes your business look hokey. Here's a rule of thumb: if you're tempted to put quotation marks around some part of the headline to help readers "get" the joke, you should remove the joke.

Jazz up your ads to maximize the impact of your message:

▶ Use color for attention! It attracts the reader's eye.

▶ Use reverse print—white letters on a black background—for sharp contrast.

▶ Use different fonts. They can make your ad unique, bring your print ads to life, and add interest.

▶ Use a photo with a punchy heading.

The completed Print Worksheet will tell you what you need to know about any publication you use. Since you may not want to do the column-inch math each time you go to buy print, it's good to have this worksheet for reference purposes. Keep all of the sheets completed by your print salespeople for fast, easy reference.

PRINT WORKSHEET
Have Your Reps Fill Out and Return This Sheet

Publication: _____

Rep's Name: _____

Phone: _____

E-Mail: _____

Publication is: ❏ Daily   ❏ Weekly   ❏ Other

Ad Size	Price	Day Ad Will Run
Full Page	$_____	_____
1/2 Page	$_____	_____
1/4 Page	$_____	_____
1/8 Page	$_____	_____
Other	$_____	_____

Special Sections Geared to This Business

Summer	Fall	Winter	Spring
_____	_____	_____	_____
_____	_____	_____	_____
_____	_____	_____	_____
_____	_____	_____	_____
_____	_____	_____	_____
_____	_____	_____	_____
_____	_____	_____	_____

Contract rate per column inch: $_____

Contract start date: _____/_____/_____   End date: _____/_____/_____

Chapter 16

Direct Mail

WHEN YOU COME HOME AT THE END OF THE WORKDAY, ONE OF the first things you do is go through your mail. While you may or may not keep everything in the pile, you definitely *look* at each piece of mail to determine what it is. On a daily basis, your bills, letters, bank statements, and magazines will almost always be accompanied by one or more pieces of direct mail in the form of individual coupons, surveys, and flyers or in envelopes stuffed with offers from many different businesses. Perhaps the irony of receiving all of these pieces of mail together has escaped you, that those direct mail pieces in your mailbox came from businesses that purchased your name and address from one or all of the *other* companies represented in that pile of mail.

Coupon Packs

First, let's look at the coupons and offers you receive in envelopes every month from national mailers like Valpak and Carol Wright. These coupon packs, referred to as *cooperative direct mail*, are sent to specific ZIP codes through local and national direct mail companies. These envelopes are stuffed full of colorful coupon offers from 30 or 40 businesses and go out to certain ZIP codes on a specific monthly schedule. They offer budget-friendly production packages in one-color to four-color printing on glossy or non-glossy paper. The paper is offered in white or color and you can have one or both sides of your coupon printed. Your quoted price should include design, layout, proof, typesetting, insertion, labels, envelopes, and postage. Your total cost will depend on the production choices you make and how many areas you wish to cover with the mailing.

While this grouping of coupons may not be your absolute first choice, mailing this way does have one advantage: it allows you to send out greater numbers of coupons and cover more areas for less money than you can by doing your own individual mailing. The practical price you pay is that the recipients who actually *keep and open* the envelopes will have to sort through all of the other material to find your piece. You also must be aware that many ZIP codes are made up of clusters of high-, middle-, and low-income dwellers as well as businesses. Depending on your offering, large percentages of the mailing may not end up in the hands of your narrowly defined targeted consumer. For this reason, this type of mailing works for products and services with wide appeal. These great little "missiles of the mail" can help increase traffic in your store.

To use this form of direct mail, you must get hold of the current schedule of each company to see which month(s) will cover the ZIP codes you want. Your reps from these companies will be happy to fax, mail, or drop by with their schedules.

If these envelopes in your area have a "window" in the front, you can buy the window placement. In other words, a portion of your coupon would show through the window for the recipients to see *before* they open the envelope. If you have your coupon designed so that the section showing through the window is very clever or teases the person into opening the envelope, you're going to get a higher rate of return on your investment because more people will at least read your mailing. The company reps will help you design your coupons for the window and show you samples to spark your imagination. It will cost a little more to buy the window position, but it is definitely worth it if you handle it right! Above all, it's the *offer itself* that becomes so important in this type of direct mail attempt.

This cooperative form of direct mail:

▶ Can give you higher volume of pieces mailed at an affordable price.

▶ Can more closely resemble an individual mailing with a great design in the window.

Historically, these types of coupon mailings work better for lower-priced items that appeal to a wide audience, such as dry cleaners, pizza and wings, car washes, lawn and garden shops, restaurants, rug or home cleaning, driveway installation and repair, etc. Free appraisal coupons work well for real estate and remodeling companies, hardwood floor installation, and the like.

Another option is to use a direct mail company (also called a mail house) that will design, print, and mail your own individual piece to your desired ZIP codes. They can separate residence addresses from business addresses or just blanket one or more areas so that every address within your chosen ZIP codes receives your mailing.

Direct mail of this sort is available in postcard-size to larger, very fancy pieces with several pages or panels and you can mail them whenever you like, without having to wait for a predetermined schedule. Although it costs more to mail this way, because many of the costs are fixed, such as postage, paper, and printing, the advantages may be worth it to you. Not only do you have control over the timing of the mailing, but your message or offer will not be put into an envelope to compete with other messages and offers: you have exclusivity.

You may find that, dollar for dollar, you enjoy better results with targeted direct mail—especially if you can combine it with radio or television.

You may find that, dollar for dollar, you enjoy better results with targeted direct mail—especially if you can combine it with radio or television. When you do, get your mailing out slightly ahead of your electronic advertising or right at the same time. Your commercials should alert radio and TV audiences to check their mail for the coupons or offers. Let them know when they can expect to receive them and what the benefit of those coupons will be.

Jon Roska, CEO of Roska Direct in Philadelphia, PA (*www.roskadirect.com*), provides us with a more personal form of direct mail:

Write a letter to your prospective customers. It should be at least two pages long. List every feature of your product or business, with the benefit to the prospect of each feature. And ask for their business or order. Mail a minimum of five letters a day, every day, five days a week, every week for a minimum of one year. (It can be more, but keep it reasonable, to what you can handle.) Small businessmen who have taken my advice over the years have seen consistent results and some, huge successes. This works, but requires discipline.

Your Offer

One would think that the best coupon offers equal the best responses, but if your offer is too good, you may not retain the customer after the offer expires. Lots of people will visit or call you for a *free* something, but the probability is high that you may never see them again. Fewer people will respond to a lesser offer, but chances are better that they are a higher quality of customer who will stay with you longer and you will have the opportunity to make them aware of other products or services you can offer them over a period of time. These customers are people with whom you can build brand loyalty.

Think about what your offer is saying, the prices you are offering, the people you want to reach, and make your choice. Understand your delivery deadline and get your offers out on time!

If you are doing a direct mail campaign, divide up the list into convenient segments and test a different offer with each segment. Once you have determined which offer works best, use that one to mail to the larger group. The same logic can be applied to other media, such as newspaper or radio ads. Test different messages and different offers. Then use the one that is most effective.

If you are doing a direct mail campaign, divide up the list into convenient segments and test a different offer with each segment.

Direct mail companies work from lists compiled from several sources to break down their targets by ZIP code and can eliminate business addresses if you only want to reach residences. They can provide you with information such as income, number of children, and education levels. Your direct mail company has vast resources when it comes to obtaining lists compiled according to the habits of individuals, such as magazine subscriptions, club memberships, store purchases, and even from credit reporting services, which will sell lists of people according to how many credit cards they have and how quickly (or slowly) they pay their bills! This information is reliable, because it has been gathered according to what people do without thinking, according to how they live their lives. When getting ready to do a local mailing, use your knowledge of your community and mail to those ZIP codes you feel will supply the best response to your product and offer.

It's a given that any mailing list has a certain percentage of outdated or invalid addresses. People move, die, or change their surnames through marriage. For whatever reason, no list will be accurate by the time it's typed, let alone printed and sold to you. Normal response to a good direct mail piece is only about 1 percent to 2 percent, so there's not much point sending out only a small number of pieces.

You will have no response at all if you make any of the following mistakes:

▶ If you target the wrong people with the wrong list, they will ignore your piece.

▶ If the design/layout doesn't attract the attention of the recipients, they won't open it.

▶ If the piece itself is not motivational or clear enough, they will toss it.

▶ If the offer is badly timed, it will have no value for them.

Ask yourself these questions:

▶ What is the product's benefit to the consumer? What need or desire does the product fill? Are you emphasizing that benefit in the ad clearly and in a strong way?

▶ How is the product superior to that of your competitors? Is it higher quality? Less expensive? More convenient to buy or use? Is it one of a kind? Are you stressing those advantages or conveniences in the ad as reasons for consumers to come to you instead of to a competitor?

▶ Does the product have a season or a window of opportunity in which the most purchases are likely to occur? An example would be snow skis, boats, or lawnmowers. Are you properly timing your mailing so you don't miss the season? Or is the product one usually purchased as needed, such as a car or a major appliance?

▶ Can your product be purchased and used at any time? If so, are you including a motivator, like a coupon or a gift with purchase for immediate use? If your product is not a high-ticket item, you may have better luck using a ZIP code mailing service such as Valpak or Carol Wright, which are both reasonably priced and do mailings to local geographical areas all year long.

To help ensure success:

▶ Include a testimonial or indicate that references from satisfied customers are available.

▶ Repeat your ad. You need to be consistent in your advertising, whatever form of media you use.

▶ Ask your sales reps to help with layout and design. It should be a free service when you purchase ad space from them.

Following these tips can help you see more customers calling, visiting your web site, or knocking at your door.

Direct Mail and "Mail Back" Offers

Reply sections of your mailings or inserts can be easily designed for people who are interested in making an appointment, receiving a free estimate, taking advantage of a discount, or entering a contest by filling in their name and address and mailing the card back to you.

This type of mailing works well for all businesses with one or more locations, for high-end retail and specialty stores, and for business-to-business material. Catalogues, brochures, and postage-paid response cards can all be specifically targeted for you with direct mail. When you send out postage-paid response cards, you pay return postage only on the pieces you get back. You can use this method of advertising as an introduction for a new business or service or to open doors for sales calls. Check your Yellow Pages under Advertising—Direct Mail for help with this kind of mailing.

Whatever kind of direct mail you use, put a lot of thought into its design and content. Consider the fact that you have only two to four seconds to get the reader's attention. Think about what kind of coupons you like to receive. Do you look at those printed on colorful paper with black lettering? What coupon offers are you more likely to hang onto and use? Turn your thoughts to your customer and decide what kind of an offer will provide enough motivation to keep him or her reading. Once you decide, repeat the offer three or four times.

Immediacy is important! The shorter the offer period is, the faster you will realize a response. Remember to put an end date on all of your mailings. If you don't give your offers a definite limit, you will find yourself honoring them for the rest of your business life.

There are many dramatic and clever combinations with color, fonts, and graphics you can use to create a direct mail piece that will catch the recipients' eye or make them curious about the rest of the message. Don't let yours be one that they pass by or throw out with nothing more than a glance because it looks flat or has too many words on it. Listen to the advice of your rep, who does this for a living. Use the experience he or she brings to your project.

And, as with everything else, make sure your logo is on every piece of direct mail you send out, along with your address, phone and fax numbers,

TIP: Save postage by inserting information on upcoming sales, new products or services, or special events to current customers in their monthly invoice envelopes.

129

TIP: If your print ads, coupons, and direct mail pieces are aimed at the older population (45+), use a slightly larger print than you normally would.

TIP: If you include a self-addressed stamped return envelope with every invoice you mail, your clients will pay their bills faster.

URL, and business hours. Request a proof of your ad before it hits the mail and check it carefully to be sure all of the information is correct. Don't leave anything to chance. Check, check, and check again.

Coupons and other types of direct response mail are some of the best types of advertising for tracking results. It is a very common practice for business owners to ask customers where they heard about the business. That's a mistake, for three reasons. One, the customer who has come into your store for a particular reason does not want to be sidetracked by that sort of a question. Two, quite honestly, you should not *want* to sidetrack that customer from looking for something to purchase. Three, the customer does not realize how important the answer is and will likely say the first thing that comes to mind ("the Yellow Pages" or "the newspaper" are the two most common answers) so he or she can get on with the business at hand.

With coupons or mail-backs, you will know *exactly* where the coupons came from. If you are using more than one publication for your inserts, have an identifying mark or change the wording or the offer slightly so you know immediately where the redeemed coupons are coming from.

When filled out by your rep(s), the Direct Mail Worksheet will provide the details you need to know to make an informed decision *before* you agree to this type of campaign and those that will be hard to remember after the fact.

Direct Mail Worksheet

Company Name _____ Sales Rep _____

Address _____ Phone _____

Fax _____ E-mail _____

❏ Group Mailing   ❏ Individual Mailing   ❏ Inserts

❏ Single-Sided   ❏ Double-Sided   ❏ Folded

Number of pieces _____ Size of piece _____

How many colors/which colors? _____

If inserts, name of publication _____ Publication date _____

Insertion cost per thousand $_____

Postage cost if mailing $_____ Mailing date _____

ZIP codes/areas covered _____

Deadline for final design and copy _____/_____/_____

Date of proof _____/_____/_____ Changes made _____

_____

_____

Final approval date _____/_____/_____

Total cost (including postage or insertion charge, tax, etc.) $_____

Title of this direct mail campaign _____

Offer or sale _____

End date on offer _____/_____/_____

Chapter 17

The Internet

YOUR COMPUTER CAN BECOME AN IMPORTANT SOURCE OF INFORMA-tion for opening, operating, and growing a successful small business. The ability to find work in faraway places has been a real boon for many small business owners and a savings oppor-tunity for companies in large cities that can fill their needs using companies in smaller cities, especially for services. Event planners, freelance writers, printers, web consultants, and graphic design companies are among small businesses that have doubled or tripled their business with contracts issued over the net from large cities across the country or around the globe.

There is so much material on the Internet you could never hope to access all of it. But you can quickly check out web addresses you find in interest-ing business magazine articles and on business-related television programs for a bit of relevant information you might otherwise not stumble upon.

For example, the Small Business Administration's web site (*www.sba.gov*) will provide you with a wealth of information on many top-ics such as how to start a home-based business, where to find start-up financing, incubator programs, counseling, exporting, conferences, and training programs and the addresses, phone numbers, and fax numbers of local Small Business Administration offices all over the United States. Links from this site also provide toll-free numbers to SBA services, programs, trade fairs, seminars, and marketing advice.

And you can use the Internet as an invaluable research tool. Check out the web sites of your competitors to see what they're up to!

Along with accessing this type of functional information, you may also wish to introduce the world to your business and attract customers and clients no matter how far away they may be. For that, you must design a basic business web site.

"If you look at just about any business card these days, you'll likely see their e-mail address along with the ubiquitous 'www' followed by their web site address," says Rachel Weingarten, President and co-founder of GTK Marketing Group in Brooklyn, New York (*www.gtkgroup.com*).

It's possible to run a successful business without having a web site, but why should you? Your web site can provide people with instant access to your company's services, contact information, success rate, and virtual media kit. You'll save time by not having to answer questions over and over when the information is accessible to anyone with a modem. You'll also be able to reach people around the globe with your company message and slogan—even while you sleep.

Your web site can provide people with instant access to your company's services, contact information, success rate, and virtual media kit.

Whether you have a significant budget or none at all, there are several factors to keep in mind when setting up your web presence. Before you go about researching web design companies, hosting services, or registering your domain, ask yourself the following questions:

▶ *Why do you want to have a web site?* Is it because everyone else seems to have one? Do you want to reach the millions of people regionally, nationally, and internationally who may be interested in learning about your company online? Is it for vanity purposes? Will you be providing content or proprietary information either for free or for a monthly fee? Is it just for fun or do you plan on augmenting your income through your web site?

▶ *What do you want your web site to accomplish?* Will it be for promotional purposes, to convey your brand messages and ideals in yet another medium? Will it be for convenience, so that anyone searching for your contact information can access it instantly at any time of the day or night? Are you planning to sell your product(s) online?

▶ *Who do you want to reach with your web site?* Will your web site provide existing customers with access to your company information even after working hours? Will you be trying to reach new and potential customers? Will you have an interactive community forum where people can exchange ideas and information?

▶ *What is your budget?* Though it's important to factor in the out-of-pocket expenses that go into creating and maintaining your web presence, including the cost of registering a domain, monthly hosting charges, and maintenance fees, it's also important to take time and energy into account as well. Will your web site be a static presence, or will it be updated daily/weekly/monthly? Will you be maintaining the web site on your own, or will you hire someone to run it for you, either in-house or through an interactive agency?

Hopefully after you answer these questions you will have a clearer idea of why you want a web site, what you want it to do, and how much money you can spend to do it. But how do you get started?

For a really basic utilitarian web site, you can register for a free web site at sites like Angelfire, Tripod, or Yahoo Sitebuilder, which provide you with templates for creating the most basic of web sites. Add a few graphics and you're done. While these are ideal for personal or fan web sites, they can be less than impressive for a business presence.

You don't have to spend a fortune to have an impressive web site, but you do need to have a really clear idea of what you want your web site to be.

You can go the extra mile by registering a web address or URL (Uniform Resource Locator), which is basically the address that people type into their web browser to reach your web site. You'll have to be creative when doing this, since there are already millions of web sites in existence and millions more going live every day of the week. You can register your URL at a site like GoDaddy.com, which will charge you about $7.95 annually for the domain. Unfortunately you can never really own your domain name, so you'll have to keep renewing every year to ensure that you keep it. Don't go for the unusual spelling when choosing a URL, since you want it to be something that people remember easily and don't have to struggle with. Your best bet is to combine two words that express your company or brand, in as short or easy a name as you can think of.

After you've registered your name you can use a web authoring tool such as Microsoft FrontPage or Macromedia Dreamweaver to actually build your web site. These authoring tools contain templates and fairly simple instructions to allow you to build a functional web site on your own. There are numerous web sites in existence that offer free graphics and fonts for you to download and add to your web site for a more personal touch.

You can go to a professional to create a clean, concise, competitive web presence. You don't have to spend a fortune to have an impressive web site, but you do need to have a really clear idea of what you want your web site to be. Your web site is a tool, in the same way that a business card is, in which you can exchange your information with others to encourage and solicit new business. Unlike a simple business card or brochure, your web site can grow along with your business and evolve as your business does. Your web site can also do business 24 hours a day, seven days a week, 365 days a year. In other words, you may be encouraging sales while you sleep.

As with most things, it's always good to get recommendations. So, if and when you decide that you're ready to hire a web design firm, first ask friends or business colleagues for referrals. Surf the net and find sites similar to your business. Study the details of their design. Do they present the look and feel and image that you'd like your business to convey? Bookmark these sites to refer to when you're ready to build your own site.

So, if and when you decide that you're ready to hire a web design firm, first ask friends or business colleagues for referrals.

Get out a pen and paper and try to answer as many of these questions as you can. By the time you're done you'll have a clear understanding of the bare bones of your web site.

1. *Create a company profile.* Who are you? What does your company do? When was your company formed and what sector do you serve? You've just created the initial "about us" page.

2. *What is your current place in the marketplace?* Are you a start-up, existing corporation, mom-and-pop shop? Your web site doesn't have to reflect where you are as a business, but you may want to convey the newness, success level, or quaintness of your brand through your site. Much in the way that many people who wish to move up the corporate level dress for the next level, your web site can convey an impression of being much larger or much cozier, depending on the audience that you'd like to attract and retain.

3. *What are your existing brand icons, logos, and slogans and how will these come into play on your web site?* Do you want your web site to reflect your company to date, or will this provide an entirely new direction for your company? Bear in mind that for branding and recognition purposes your interest would be best served if you have consistent look, feel, and design elements on all collateral materials, including the web. So, if you're looking to redesign your brand, you should continue this through to your business card, stationery, packaging, etc.

4. *Define success in relationship to this project.* How will you know if this web site is a success? What will you do if it fails?

Some additional tips to keep in mind when creating your web site are:

▶ *Simple is better.* Avoid bells and whistles. For the most part, people have dial-up modems and don't have cutting-edge computers. Avoid bogging down their systems with unnecessary components, animations, and large graphics files. They may get frustrated with your slow-loading site and leave before the entire page loads. Opt for clean design with minimal graphics, unless you're a magazine site or shopping site.

▶ *Clear, easy navigation systems.* Build a clear and simple navigation system and have it in the same place on every page—either at the top or bottom of the page, preferably both. The most common elements in a navigation system are Home (with a link to your home page), About Us (your chance to tell them about your company in a nutshell), Press or Testimonials (where you can wow them with your press clippings or raves from clients), FAQ or frequently asked questions (save a lot of time and energy by giving people answers to the most frequently asked questions about your business), Contact Us (it's important to have contact information on every page, even if it's just a catchall e-mail address that is checked frequently).

▶ *Keep your language clear and easy.* Most movies last an hour and a half, since most people have a really short attention span. That's even shorter online. Offer up "byte-size" versions of your corporate message and business.

▶ *Services/Shop.* Don't forget to tell them what you do and give them clear, easily accessible links to buy your products.

▶ *Follow up.* If someone contacts you by e-mail, follow up their query. You never know where the next business lead will come from.

▶ *Evolve.* Don't just create your web site and forget about it. Add news about your company, your accomplishments, and timely events. Give people a reason to keep visiting your site.

▶ *Register your web site on search engines.* You'd be amazed at how many people find web sites through Google and the rest. Register your web site at *www.dmoz.org*, which is a web directory and something like a huge reference library of web addresses that hundreds of search engines, including Netscape Search, AOL Search, Google, Lycos, HotBot, and DirectHit, refer to.

Whatever you do, realize that a web site is not etched in stone. Your site can grow and evolve as your company does.

Before actually developing the web site, you will have to do some preparation. You must determine what the format of your web site will be, how much and what text it will contain, whether or not you will use graphics or music in your presentation, and how many pages the site will hold. Be sure you set up your site so that it flows from page to page and links are provided so that visitors can get from one section to another quickly and easily. Make additions to your page occasionally, so that it remains fresh and interesting to visitors who return. Check your site often and, whenever you make changes, always activate the spell-check function. Keep it simple but compelling. Clutter doesn't convey the right message. Banner advertising works well for portal sites, but is of questionable value to small sites.

There are a lot of web sites and a lot of competitors. Give your customers a reason to visit you. Special offers, available only to web visitors, work well. Mention your web site in all communication with your customers. Put the URL on your business cards (yes, throw the old ones away!), on any newspaper ads, correspondence, flyers, direct mail, and any other venue you choose to use.

The web site should be reflective of the image (brand) you wish to create. If you have a conservative business, a flashy web site might not project the image you wish to convey. Rob Cherof of BBDO in Atlanta, says,

> Before you build your web site, figure out what you want to accomplish. Like any medium, it can be great, or it can be awful. The key is defining what you want it to do before you design it.

Whether you decide to do it yourself or find help, you will need to draw your site out on paper before it goes on the computer. Start with a circle in the center of a sheet of paper and label it "Home Page." On another piece of paper, list the names of all of the pages you will want visitors to be able to access. Go back and surround the center "Home Page" with a circle for every page you listed and draw a line from each circle back to the center circle. Label each one.

There are a lot of web sites and a lot of competitors. Give your customers a reason to visit you. Special offers, available only to web visitors, work well.

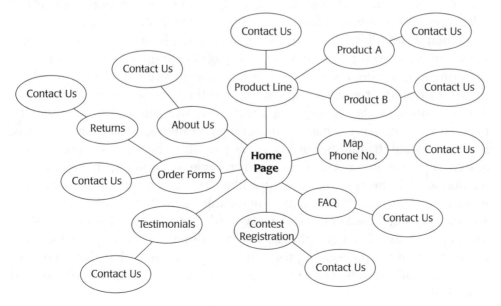

Work outward from those basic circles. You should have an e-mail link from every page and a navigation bar that will allow someone to go to any other page from anywhere on your site.

Once your site is finished, refer to your original drawing to be sure you've created all the pages and links you wanted. Then click on all of the links to be sure they're working. Do that at least once a week, or even once a day for a really busy site. On your home page, remind visitors to book-mark your site so that they can return easily.

You can submit your URL (www address) to individual search engines by filling out a basic form usually found near the bottom of search engine home pages.

You can submit your URL (www address) to individual search engines by filling out a basic form usually found near the bottom of search engine home pages like *www.mamma.com* and *www.google.com/addurl.html.* Look for "Add URL" or "Add Site" or "Suggest a Site." *www.submitit.com* or *www.sitescreamer.com* will submit your site to the more than 2,000 search engines for a fee. These services often submit your sites several times over a period of 12 months.

Why would your site need to be submitted more than once? Because it will not always be picked up by all (or any) of the search engines on the first, the second, or even the third try. Occasionally, you should make some changes to your site, not only to keep visitors interested, but because search engines will perceive your site to be abandoned or inactive if it stays the same for long periods of time and discard it to make room for others. Check periodically to see if your site has been listed on each search engine, by typing your URL into each engine's search box. But keep in mind that it can take weeks, even months, for your listing to appear after you submit it.

When a search engine visits your site, it reads and records all of the words on your web pages. If your web pages contain a specific word that someone is searching for as a keyword, then your site will show up high on the list of results. If you sign up with one of the URL submitting companies that I mentioned above, they will check your site and make recommendations so your site has the best chance of a high ranking for certain keywords. It's best to keep the number of keywords you list to between six and 10. The search engine won't sweep your site forever when coming up with search results, so pick the ones that are most likely to make your site pop up. Keep in mind that the term "keywords" can include phrases, not just single words. So you may put "teachers" in as a keyword, but you can also put in "K-12 lesson plans" as a keyword phrase. The best thing to do is to put yourself in the mindset of people looking for your site and decide what they may type into a keyword search. They may type in "How to publish a book" or just "publishing."

You can also do a search for companies similar to yours and visit the sites that rank in the top 10 spots. Once on their homepages, find a clear spot (where your cursor remains in the arrow shape) and then right-click your mouse. Go to "View Source" and the site's keywords will be revealed. This will give you a good idea about what keywords to use. Of course, those keywords must show up frequently in the text of your own web site as well.

Sharron Senter, a Boston-based marketing consultant specializing in helping businesses increase search engine traffic and web site profits (*www.sharronsenter.com*), says:

It's imperative in today's business environment to maintain a web site, no matter what products or services you sell. There's no overstating the necessity. A web site is your electronic business card. You wouldn't be caught dead at a networking event or in front of a prospect without a business card, nor should you be without a web site, or you'll leave the impression that you're not very serious about your business.

However, it's not enough to simply host a web site. In order to lure visitors to your site, you must optimize it to attract qualified search engine traffic. The process is commonly referred to as Search Engine Optimization (SEO). What's more, it costs nothing to be a magnet for search engine traffic.

Search Engine Optimization involves many steps. First, let's take a look at how search engines work and why targeting them will grow your business. Millions of people each day visit the various search engines, such as Yahoo and Google, and search for products and services they're interested in. Search engines are responsible for informing users about the masses of resources on the Internet, your web site being just one resource. It's at the time of the search when optimization efforts pay off. Specifically, if you understand what prospects will search for to find products and services such as yours, your web site's URL will be more likely returned by a search engine, thus prompting a user to click through to your web site.

Important SEO Terms:

Inbound Link—A web site hyperlinking to another web site. For example, web site A links to web site B, equaling an inbound link for B.

Keywords—Words prospects query at search engines. The same words you need to sprinkle throughout your web site.

Keyword Phrases—A string of words prospects query at search engines. Again, the same words you need to sprinkle throughout your web site.

Search Engine—A hub on the Internet where customers and prospects visit to

139

search "terms" or "words" to find information or answers to their questions.

There are several steps to optimizing your web site. Let's talk about the three most important:

Step #1—Understand Your Customers and Prospects. It's imperative you know who your target audience is, since you'll use keywords at your web site to attract prospects. If you misinterpret who your customer is, then you'll fail at search engine optimization. For example, there is a fine difference between the terms "mom" and "step mom." It may be important for your business model to differentiate between the two in order to attract a qualified audience. Step moms may refer to themselves as just that, not moms. If you don't know this, you may miss speaking to your target audience.

Step # 2—Build a Keyword-Rich Web Site. It's imperative your web site be keyword-rich, filled with words your prospects and customers search for at search engines to find products and services such as yours.

Step # 3—Build Inbound Links. One of the measurements search engines consider, when deciding what web sites to return in a search, is how popular web sites are, meaning how many inbound links are pointing to a web site. Think of an inbound link as a vote. The more inbound links you have, the more popular search engines will believe your web site to be, thus directing more traffic your way. However, you don't want just any old inbound link; you want links that are complementary to your business and also rank high with search engines. For example, if you're an accountant, you'll receive higher measurements for having an inbound link from your industry trade association, rather than from a local restaurant down the street. The latter has nothing to do with your business. To optimize your web site, you want keyword-rich web pages and as many complementary inbound links as possible. These two elements will make the greatest positive impact in your web site ranking, directing more qualified traffic to your web site.

Optimization Example

Suppose you own a gift basket business specializing in creating and delivering baby baskets. Your baskets are commonly filled with diapers, rattles, formula, etc. The first step in optimizing your web site is to generate a list of keywords and keyword phrases. To accomplish this, first list every word you believe your target audience would use at search engines to find baby gift baskets. Your list may look something like this: baby baskets, newborn gifts, baby shower gifts, new moms, new mothers, baby gifts, gifts for baby, baby shower, christening gifts, newborn gift basket ideas, baby clothes, gifts for new baby, etc.

Once you've built your list, then use these keywords often throughout your sales copy and on all of your web pages. What's more, you don't have to guess what prospects are searching for. There are many search engine monitoring tools that'll tell you exactly what people are searching for. WordTracker (*www.wordtracker.com*) is just one resource. WordTracker will tell you how often people search for certain keywords and how many competing web sites use these words. The latter is important, because you'll want to focus on words that are popular, but don't have a lot of competing pages. For example, suppose the keyword phrase "baby gift baskets" is searched 1,200 times a day and there are a total of 975 competing web pages using this keyword phrase. You'll do far better in the search engines if you use "preemie baby baskets" since there are 85 daily searches, but only three competing web pages. Remember that you only need a minuscule portion of search engine traffic to be flooded with qualified visitors.

The most important step in optimizing any web site is knowing who your audience is.

The most important step in optimizing any web site is knowing who your audience is. If you miss this step, then your sales copy and keywords will miss their target. Search engines want to give top ranking to a web site that is the best match to an individual search query. Keep this in mind and you'll optimize successfully.

Are You the Registrant of Your Own Domain?

If you hire a company or an individual to create your site for you, be sure that you are listed as the registrant of your domain name. If you don't, the company or individual you hired may list themselves as registrant and will have complete control over your domain name and perhaps hold you up for lots of money to transfer it over to you if you part ways. So have that understanding up front—and get it in writing. Getting a domain's registrant changed is like getting out of a bad marriage: if you can avoid the situation in the first place, you'll save an enormous amount of stress and money later.

If you've already had a site done by someone else, you can check it out by going to *www.networksolutions.com* and click on "WHOis" after you type in your domain name. You will be taken to an information page that shows you the name of the registrant, the technical contact person, and other information. If the registrant isn't you, you may be in trouble. Unfortunately, it's a subject not many people know to broach upfront, and web design companies don't usually mention it.

A web design company will probably give you a couple of different payment packages to choose from. One choice will include a hosting fee and either to create a new web site or to take over and maintain a current web

141

site (make changes, additions, etc.). This choice means that your domain name will most likely be registered through their business, so reread the previous two paragraphs before you choose this path. The second choice will be to simply charge an hourly fee or a retainer fee to update and maintain the site. This may cost you more in the long run, because if you don't know *what* they're doing, you won't know how long it should take them to do it. It's one of the difficult circumstances computer-challenged people find themselves in!

If you are not a computer expert, or you don't have the time or inclination to even search out software to help you design the pages of a web site, contact your local SBA office or Chamber of Commerce.

Your domain name and your web site are two different animals, so you should also have a written agreement that the site content will be turned over to you upon request without penalty or you could end up paying to have someone else do it all over again.

If you are not a computer expert, or you don't have the time or inclination to even search out software to help you design the pages of a web site, contact your local SBA office or Chamber of Commerce and ask if they can recommend someone who creates web sites for a living. You may find a fellow entrepreneur who is just getting started and will give you a good price in exchange for recommending him or her to others. Or get a kid to do it for you. My teenage son is a computer fiend and he has developed a ton of web sites for himself, for his friends, and a local business, and he designed two of my web sites. I paid him, of course, but I would have had to pay a lot more to a professional—and I love the work he does. If you don't have access to a teenage computer whiz, contact your local high school and ask the computer teacher to recommend someone. Or ask a niece or nephew to recommend a friend. This is also the perfect opportunity for that intern to help you out!

Hosting

There are places that offer free hosting, but you have to promote them in some way on your site—usually with a banner on your home page and you can't control what they put on it. If you don't care about that, go for it. But hosting isn't that expensive—usually $9 to $19 a month, a nominal fee for looking professional. More importantly, it's not a lot to pay for what you really want from a hosting company—unparalleled customer service.

Think of your web site in three ways:

As a location to do business. If you sell from your site, understand that people who shop this way want to be able to complete the process online. They don't want to get to the point of purchase and then have to call an 800-number or send a check to a P.O. box. While checks and cash work as well as credit cards in your brick-and-mortar locations, they're not as effective on the Net. The ability to accept credit cards gives you the opportunity to make an immediate sale rather than having someone print out an order form, fill it out, and snail mail it to you with a check. That gives the customer too much time be distracted before the task is complete or to change his or her mind and not follow through with the purchase at all. And customers, especially Internet people, want their purchases to arrive as soon as possible. They know that you will wait for their check to clear before you send them the goods and they will be turned off by what they view as a long, primitive process.

When choosing a company to set you up for e-commerce, be sure and ask how often they check for bad or stolen credit cards. Some companies check every so many weeks; some check every few minutes. You may pay a little more for a company like BankCard USA (*www.takecards.com*)—one that checks for bad or stolen cards constantly, deposits funds into your account quickly, and provides customer service 24 hours a day in 21 languages. But if these things are important to you, it's worth the extra cost.

As an inexpensive and unlimited form of advertising. Even if you won't be selling anything from your site, you need to have a web presence to show your local clients that you are on top of things and using up-to-date technology. Lots of people in your market browse the Net for shopping or for information purposes and you want them to see you there. They may want to check your site for your hours or sale information, track an item they've ordered from you, or ask a question about a product you carry or a service you offer.

Even if you won't be selling anything from your site, you need to have a web presence to show your local clients that you are on top of things and using up-to-date technology.

You can design your web site to include anything and everything with no thought to production costs associated with talent, postage, printing costs, camera crews, etc. and you can add words, subtract words, or otherwise alter every word at will.

As a way to add a new revenue stream. Use your site to add diversity to your business by making contacts that will allow you to write online articles, find new products to sell or new services to provide, look for business from out-of-state or even out-of-country clients from sites like *www.profnet.com*.

If you are selling product on your site, be sure that people can return items they're not satisfied with. Returns are a problem that Internet companies are wrangling with. Some are hiring companies that do nothing but handle returns while others are trying to do it themselves by having items purchased on the Net returned to their brick-and-mortar locations. Even though you may not be a giant yet, your customers have to be happy with their shopping experience at your site or they won't come back.

It is important to develop a solid and generous return policy. (Be sure yours is displayed in plain sight, both in your store and on your web site.) This is such an important part of retaining customers that I wanted to share my very favorite return policy, on or off the web, with you. It can be seen in True Value Hardware Stores:

> If it doesn't match,
> fit, go up, go down,
> tighten, loosen,
> screw, unscrew,
> or just isn't the
> thing-majig you wanted,
> bring it back!

Reprinted with permission of TruServ Corporation

Get 'Em, Keep 'Em, Get 'Em, Keep 'Em ...

Devising ways of getting visitors to your site, keeping them there, and figuring out how to get them to return will keep you up all night.

Devising ways of getting visitors to your site, keeping them there, and figuring out how to get them to return will keep you up all night, just like it keeps radio and television executives up. Why? Because now you're doing the same job they do, on top of the job you already have. In the good old pre-net days, business owners didn't have to think about *being* a form of media. They simply "minded the store" and left it to the media to lure and keep audiences, so that when it was time to advertise, their target market was ready and waiting. But now, on the web, you have to create and keep your *own* audience as well as mind the store.

In the past few years, the American public has been swamped with direct mail, print ads, TV commercials, and just about any other form of advertising you can think of. The web is the one resource that started from a real need to access and review information, where ordinary people have all of the control. They decide what's worth watching, reading, researching, and, most importantly, buying. If they can get to the information quickly and solve a problem or answer a question, the more they'll come back. It's that easy.

But so often the first fatal mistake companies make when building a web site is not getting their wary target audience involved. Rarely do companies spend time watching and questioning their users. In their haste to get some-thing—anything—up and running, they rush around and, before they know it, they've spent too much money to create and build a web site that doesn't satisfy the needs of the user. Whether it's content-driven or a commerce site, the user will tell you what works and what doesn't. From the navigation, to page clicks, to the flow of information, to the content, users need to be involved in the process.

The web site should be created with the visitors in mind, that it's meant to solve a problem for them. For example, the easier it is for someone to find parenting information or to quickly order a birthday gift, the more "sticky" the site will become and the better chance the company will have to culti-vate new users. Word-of-mouth is important in building your site.

The web site should be created with the visitors in mind, that it's meant to solve a problem for them.

You can create a mailing list from such contacts and use it as an avenue to make future contacts with new information or a deal. Always ask, on your first contact, if visitors would like to receive more information, as it becomes available, or a monthly newsletter from you. Those who want that contact from you will become a mailing list that you can use as a base; it will grow if you keep your site interesting, entertaining, and informative. Always provide a way for the recipients to opt out of receiving your e-mails going forward.

Most times people will click on an interesting link without realizing that they're providing you with personal information as well as their e-mail address. If you're sending them free stuff, you obviously need their name and address. How many times have you provided personal information to receive a free sample, subscribe to a newsletter, or enter a contest? This is how e-mail lists are built (and then sold). This is how you end up on Internet mailing lists as surely as you end up on those that find you through the postal service.

Post a privacy policy explaining what you do, and do not do, with the addresses you collect. People want to know, before identifying themselves, exactly what you intend to do with their e-mail addresses.

Advertising on the Web

Rosemary Brisco, who earlier told us about writing for online portals and trade publications, tells us that search engines offer "pay-per-click" (PPC) ad space where you create a short text ad and associate it with specific words that your customers are likely to use when searching for your products and services.

You only pay when a prospect clicks on your ad and is taken to your web site. This is highly cost-effective and has the advantage of "prequalifying" your prospects because they have expressed interest in what your ad offers. All major search engines such as Google and Overture offer PPC advertising. The cost of click-throughs starts as low as five cents per click with the high side around two dollars per click. It all depends on the search engine you choose and your positioning.

Brisco provides this quick-start guide:

► Identify the words that your prospects use to find your products. An easy-to-use search term suggestion tool is available at *www.inventory. overture.com.*

► Create your text ad based on the guidelines at the search engine you've chosen.

► Determine your monthly or daily budget for each ad campaign.

► Monitor your ad campaigns. Keep track of what works and what doesn't. Use the "Reports" feature to adjust your ads as needed.

"And," says Brisco, "don't be taken in by the plethora of free 'Add a Site' services that claim to raise your web site visibility in their search engine. The web has become too crowded for this to be effective. With PPC advertising, you have a much higher probability of being found in the search engines."

Whatever your business is, you need a web site. If you intend to do it "someday," but not immediately, at least check to see if the domain name you want is available and get it registered now. You can reserve a name even if you are not ready to complete the site.

Only a couple of years ago, an Internet presence was something to think about, but there was no real urgency associated with it. Today, a business is considered archaic without one.

Getting on the Internet is an important part of opening your business. Only a couple of years ago, an Internet presence was something to think about, but there was no real urgency associated with it. Today, a business is considered archaic without one.

Be Patient, but Don't Relax!

It will take time to build your web-based business, especially if you don't have a brick-and-mortar location to play off of. Combination locations, called "click-and-brick," make it easier to get people who are already familiar and happy with your business to your web site and make things like returning product easier.

At this writing, I would say it could take a good five years to build up your e-business, but that shouldn't surprise anyone. It takes time to build any business. Just because everything on the web is fast, click here, click there, people have the notion that plopping a web site on the Internet means instant business, instant wealth. It just isn't so. But don't let that keep you from working your butt off from day one. You may be able to shorten that five-year estimate and you'll need to put a lot of early effort into keeping your site fresh, updated, convenient, informative, and reliable!

Getting a Sponsor for Your Web Page

Profits from your web site can come in more ways than one. Your site can be a place where people come for information or advice on a particular subject or to interact with people interested in the same hobby, career, or interests, as well as to purchase something.

What you look for here is a company willing to sponsor your site. In other words, a company that is willing to pay to advertise on your site because the people who visit your site are the very people it wants to reach. Your site becomes a marketing tool for their company by providing a link from your site to theirs.

Is Your Site Advertiser-Worthy?

Advertisers determine the value of radio and television stations and publications by the size of their audiences and by the length of time individuals listen, watch, or read. The worth of your web site will be based on the same thing: How many visitors does the site register every day or every week and how long do they stay there?

You have to give visitors a reason to stay at your site, just as you would keep them in your brick-and-mortar location. Grocery stores put the milk and the video departments in the back of the store for the same reason as Borders puts coffee shops in its bookstores—to keep people in the stores longer. It's all about bringing in new visitors, keeping them longer, and proving that you can keep them coming back. This is the key to an advertiser's heart.

How do you prepare to attract a sponsor?

- ► Make a list of companies that would want to reach the people who come to your site. Does your site attract small business owners, teachers, people planning weddings, antique car buffs, jewelry lovers, nature lovers, moviegoers, boating enthusiasts, brewers—who?

- ► Advertise your site through paid advertising, articles, bulletin boards,

147

message boards, shared links, etc. to increase traffic to your site. Any company that would consider spending money to sponsor your site will want to know how many people visit the site daily, weekly, and monthly and from where. Sites like *www.sitetracker.com* will track your visitors for a small fee.

▶ When you've built up your web site and have achieved constant high visitor numbers, write or e-mail a proposal to one or more of the companies you think would like to advertise to your visitors. Either design one proposal for a single company to sponsor the entire site or divide up your site and sell sections of it to different (noncompeting) companies.

▶ Write up a contract spelling out the terms of the sponsorship (length of sponsorship and price, terms of payment, etc.) and have it checked by a contract attorney before sending it out for a signature.

▶ Continue improving, updating, and advertising your site to keep your visitor numbers up—that will be a condition of the agreement the sponsor will insist on. After all, he or she will not want to spend money on a site that will have no management or continuing effort behind it.

How Do You Do? Who Are You?

Once you get people coming to your site, how do you find out who they are? How do you get back to them? That's one of the biggest frustrations of the Internet.

Once you get people coming to your site, how do you find out who they are? How do you get back to them? That's one of the biggest frustrations of the Internet. People can slip in and out and leave no trail … and even the tracking services I mentioned previously, that can track visitors' countries, list referring web pages, and tell you what search engines were used to find your site, can't grab the e-mail addresses of your visitors. But you can trap some of those slippery visitors into giving up their e-mail addresses if you provide an interesting link to your site for them to click on:

▶ To win a prize
▶ To give an opinion
▶ To get the "joke of the day"
▶ To get something free
▶ To receive your monthly e-newsletter

Use an e-mail link to open a dialogue with your visitors. On my own business web site, *www.silentpartneradvertising.com*, I answer advertising questions for free. This gives me a chance to talk one-on-one with small business owners or people thinking about opening a business, people I would never come into contact with face-to-face.

Michael Sevilla, President of Gravity Metrics (*www.gravitymetrics.com*) in Denver, Colorado, says:

> If someone told you that they were considering your product/service, but needed some information before they decided to buy from you right now instead of your competition, wouldn't you make sure that they received the information they needed? Most companies work hard to keep existing customers and even harder to get new ones. Yet how much time and money is wasted on addressing perceived needs instead of the known needs of both existing and potential customers?
>
> Almost every company that has a web site is sitting on a gold mine of information that could reveal their customers' true needs, what is important to them, and what sales/marketing language is most effective for getting them to buy from you instead of your competition. Here's an eye-opening statistic: recent studies have shown that, on average, nearly 80 percent of potential purchasers of goods and service believe that going to a company's web site is an important part of the decision-making process. If you have a web site, what is it telling that 80 percent? If you don't have a web site, how will that negatively impact the impression of your company? Will you be perceived as "real"? Think about all those potential customers looking at your web site as they try to decide if they'll buy from you. Do you know what information is critical for them to make that decision?
>
> Let's think about your web site's visitors in a more traditional sales funnel manner. Most salespeople look at the universe and decide what type of individuals or companies might buy from them (suspects). Then, they ask themselves, who is more likely to need what I offer? By breaking down that universe into more specific groups or targets, the salesperson has just defined groups that are more likely to buy from them (prospects). From these prospects they focus again on those that have a more pressing need, and these people become qualified leads.

Nearly 80 percent of potential purchasers of goods and service believe that going to a company's web site is an important part of the decision-making process.

50,000 visitors to site	
100% of visitors	**Total visitors**
75% of visitors	**Returning visitors**
50% of visitors	**Product description**
30% of visitors	**Put items in cart**
7%	**Checkout process**
5%	**Complete transaction**

149

Well, in the web-enabled world, your web site actually knocks out a layer of the traditional sales funnel. Think about it. Everyone that comes to your web site does so voluntarily. Rather exciting to think that these visitors are specifically going to you to fulfill their needs. Somehow they were motivated to sit down, turn on a computer, find your web address, and look at your web site. Why? Because they probably considering buying from you and they want more information.

But, let's look at the other edge of the proverbial sword. Most visitors to your web site know on some level what information they are looking for. Therefore your web site should be clearly organized, copy should be concise and to the point, and use standard terms for the navigation (About Us, Contact, Products, Pricing, FAQ, Services, Testimonials, etc. navigation must be obvious and consistent throughout the site).

So let's stop for a moment and check where we are. About 80 percent of the people thinking about buying from you will probably look at your web site. The mere act of going to your web site indicates that they have some level of interest in what you have to offer. The next question: do you know what information they want? This is the critical information that will compel them to buy from you instead of your competition. Your web site is an incredible marketing tool. Not only can you quickly change your web site, but those that visit your web site are qualified leads.

And now for a bit of news that most people don't realize. Everything that happens on your web site can be tracked, measured, and analyzed.

And now for a bit of news that most people don't realize. Everything that happens on your web site can be tracked, measured, and analyzed. From this information you can determine how people found you, what marketing/sales language is most effective, and what type of information your different customer segments need to have to make a decision. Amazing stuff! Too bad most companies don't take advantage of this gold mine of information. Let's look at how you access the information, how to interpret the data, and how to put the information and insight into action.

Every web site visitor generates a history of their visit. All of these visits are compiled and stored in a web site's log files. In essence, the log files are a historical record of how each visitor interacted with your web site. Whoever is hosting your web site (e.g. hosting company, web site development company, etc.) probably has a few months of your web site's historical log files. These are usually saved on a month-by-month basis. Many hosting companies offer monthly reports that show standardized reports regarding your web site. This information varies based upon the web analytics service your web hosting company subscribes to. But, almost always you'll at least get the following information:

- ▶ Total Visits
- ▶ Total Page Views
- ▶ Total Hits
- ▶ Average Visits per Day
- ▶ Average Page Views per Day
- ▶ Average Bytes per Day
- ▶ Average Page Views per Visit
- ▶ Average Hits per Visit
- ▶ Average Length of Visit
- ▶ New Visitors
- ▶ Repeat Visitors

Now that we've found the information, what the heck does it all mean? One month's information doesn't mean too much. What really counts is how the month-over-month information trends. So, if you notice that your total number of visitors is declining and the average length of the visit is also declining, check your sales. More often, sales will have dropped within the same time frame.

Which leads me to interpreting the data and applying the information from that data. If you're fortunate enough to have access to more comprehensive reporting solutions, here are some of the areas that you should investigate:

- ▶ Top path analysis
- ▶ Key search words/phrases
- ▶ Referring URLs

Examples of how you can use this information:

1. You use your web site to showcase your work and generate sales leads. (Your web site has two goals: show examples of your work and have people contact you because they considering using your services.) Using Total Page Views, Average Page Views per Visitor, New and Repeat Visitors, let's look at how these numbers trend over three months. Do the numbers for each stay the same or fluctuate? More than likely, the numbers change month to month. Total Page Views will give you a rough idea of how much activity is on your web site. The Average Page Views per Visitor indicate how involved your visitors are with your web site. If the number is less than two, it could mean that most visitors are confused/bored/uncertain after arriving at your home page and don't know what to do next. (This assumes, of course, you have at least 10 pages to your web site.) For some reason, most visitors see or don't see something that makes them leave your web site. Let's add New and Repeat Visitors. Do you have more

New Visitors acting this way? If so, something on your web site within those first two pages is driving them away from you. Make sure your links work, your copy is clear, and you have a defined path/goal for visitors to take next (e.g., "click here for examples," "click here for more information," "click here for references"). More than likely, your visitors don't know where to go next. It's your job to lead them.

2. You sell products online. By analyzing information from the Navigational Path report, key search words/phrases, number of visitors, and your total sales, you can figure out who (Google, Yahoo, MSN, etc.) is bringing you the best traffic. Here, we define "best traffic" as those who buy from you, not just those who visit your web site.

   By working backwards, we look at the total number of people who saw your "Thanks for your purchase" page (from the Navigational Path report). We then see the pages that most of those people viewed before they saw that page. All we're doing is recreating the most popular pages viewed (and in what order) on your web site. Notice what pages people used to arrive at the "Thanks for your purchase" page. Here are the web pages that directly impact your sales. What is on those pages? Whatever it is, that information is crucial to making people buy from you.

3. Using the same report, look at the top paths. How long are they, and where do they end (at what page)? You may be losing visitors along the way to your "Thanks for your purchase" page because of something you're not providing. Look at the pages and see what topics they discuss, what those pages have in common. Is the copy clear? Are links working to the next page? Have you clearly lined out the next step you want visitors to take?

We keep looking back through the sales funnel until we arrive at your home page. Now looking at your key search words/phrases, we can see how many people from each search engine (and which search engine) came to your web site and what words they used to find you (e.g., "designer widgets," "hand-carved widget," "trade-friendly widget," etc.).

Advertise Your URL for Best Results

After all of the excitement over advertising on the Internet, it turns out that the huge dotcom companies made a name for themselves by advertising on radio, on television, and in print—the conventional forms of advertising. And now that a few of the dotcom giants are enjoying a certain comfort level in name and e-address awareness, they have become competitors of the radio, television, and print entities that made it possible for them to become giants. And they are working very hard to lure clients away from the traditional forms of advertising. Most small business owners are still wondering whether advertising, even on local web sites provided by their daily newspapers, radio, or television stations, will increase name awareness or traffic to their stores.

Like the giants, your small dotcom company will have to be promoted in traditional forms of advertising to bring clients to your web site. The banners and click-throughs still don't have much of a proven track record and the Internet is too huge (and growing) to make us feel really comfortable about shooting our money into cyberspace. In fact only about one out of 50 (to one out of 100) people actually click on a banner when they see one.

You can run classified ads in newspapers in your area, or anywhere else, using a great headline to capture the reader's attention and give your web address. Example:

> ### Save 50% on Wallpaper!
> www.cheapwallpaper.com

Use the less expensive 10-second or 15-second radio and television ads to get your web address out. Spend time browsing the Net for bulletin boards, newsgroups, and message boards where you can leave your URL and ask people to visit. Approach sites that have something in common with yours (but not competitors) and ask if they would add a link to your site from theirs if you reciprocate. Once people go to your site, you can present them with more information than you could ever provide in a radio or television commercial or print ad. So let the traditional forms of advertising help get your customers to your web site as well as to your street locations.

TIP: Keep the text portions of your web page(s) short. No one wants to read and read and read a web page. Use color, graphics, and even music to keep the page(s) interesting and the reader reading.

TIP: Search online for business-related purchases. I buy locally, but if you're not as big a sap as I am about this, you can almost always shop better online.

Chapter 18

Outdoor Advertising

OUTDOOR ADVERTISING IS BOLD, COLORFUL, AND CONSTANT AND takes the guesswork out of how to reach a specific demographic. I have often argued that if you've hung a sign outside of your business, you've already demonstrated your belief in the power of outdoor advertising. Now you have to decide how many people should see your sign—or one like it. Are the people who drive by your door every day enough or do you also need to reach people who don't normally use the road in front of your business? Obviously, you need to reach many more people than those who pass by on their way home each day.

One way to accomplish that is to take advantage of billboards placed along well-traveled routes ten to 20 miles, up to 40 to 50 miles away from your business. Billboard locations are everywhere! Outdoor billboards can be purchased close to, or a distance from, your business location(s) and extend the information on the sign over your door to more than just the people who travel back and forth in front of your store or office. Outdoor billboards can point the way to your door with specific directions, alert visitors or newcomers to the area about your business, and serve as a last-minute reminder to drivers that you carry what they need.

Demographics ... please! Outdoor billboards are perfect for any business with a customer base old enough to drive. It doesn't matter which radio stations the drivers or passengers prefer or which television programs they watch or which publications they read when they get home. None of that matters! What a relief! An enormous amount of stress is removed from trying to decide where to best spend your advertising dollars.

Do you know many people who won't be in their car or on a bus at some point today? Tomorrow? I didn't think so. You don't have to go looking for advertising that will find your customers. With outdoor, customers come to your advertising.

Lighted billboards promote your business and location up to 18 hours a day and are seen by the people who constantly drive by them, by those who only occasionally pass through the area, and by those who are lost!

Is your business web-site-oriented? You can bring traffic to your site with outdoor advertising, as shown in this example from Guy Lyman of Guy Lyman Advertising.

Outdoor billboards are perfect for any business with a customer base old enough to drive.

Billboards can be purchased by the month or on long-term contracts. They are available in several sizes, along two-lane roads as well as super-highways. You can buy a few billboards and have them moved from one location to another on a *rotary program* or you can buy groups of boards called a *showing* and have them all up at one time in various locations. A showing can offer 25%, 50%, 75%, or even 100% coverage of the daily driving public. The number of boards you need to achieve these percentages depends on your location, the number of roads leading to your location, and the number of boards you can afford. Most outdoor companies have a variety of programs to accommodate different budgets.

Why this form of advertising is growing:

▶ The expanded use of VCRs and DVD players and the fragmentation of television audiences due to the increase in the number of available stations, which makes television advertising more of a long shot.

▶ The high cost of trying to cover a specific demographic adequately on available radio stations.

▶ The dramatic cost increase many local markets experience in newspaper advertising while readership in many of those same markets is declining.

▶ The increased mobility of today's population, making highways and neighborhood roads perfect places for your message.

Like giant breadcrumbs, outdoor billboards lead customers from your advertising message they hear or see at home to their purchase at your business location.

Like giant breadcrumbs, outdoor billboards lead customers from your advertising message they hear or see at home to their purchase at your business location. And because its presence is continuous (you can't turn it off or hit a fast-forward button to get rid of it), outdoor advertising produces frequency levels unmatched by other media. Billboards truly keep your message alive long after the paper has been thrown out and the radio and television have been turned off. Billboards serve as a constant reminder to local traffic and an immediate first notice to tourists or people who have recently moved into the area.

Billboards make your small business look big! All businesses, no matter how large or small, have the same choices when it comes to billboard size. While individual boards of different sizes dot the landscape, boards that are grouped together in twos or threes along roads and highways are all the same size. So the display for your small business can look just as impressive and have the same chance of getting results as that of a corporate behemoth right next to yours. For this reason, outdoor billboards are often referred to as "the great equalizers." This cannot be said of print, where the size of a business is suggested by the size of its newspaper ad, or of the Yellow Pages, where there's a disparity in ad sizes—and where your potential customers are led to the display ads of all of your larger and more established competitors.

Outdoor billboards can also enhance your other advertising:

▶ Combine outdoor with your television spots to reach fragmented audiences and put back the impact lost by channel zappers.

▶ Combine outdoor with newspaper to not only keep your one-time print ad going all day long, but increase its size and add color to it as well.

▶ Combine outdoor with your radio schedules to add visual presence with bold graphics and the eight to ten most powerful and recognizable words of your radio copy. (The combination of radio and outdoor used to be known as "poor man's television.")

Billboards work well for specialty shops and high-ticket outdoor items like motorcycles, snowmobiles, riding lawnmowers, and automobiles, as well as tires, oil change and tune-up locations, car washes, and anything else to do with a car. After all, the customer is sitting in the vehicle that needs those new tires, is making a funny noise, or could use a good washing as he or she passes your message on the road. Perfect for that impromptu purchase.

Directional billboards are perfect for directing traffic right to your door if you can find one or more nicely located boards on which you can place your logo with an arrow and/or a directional message. This type of board is very helpful if you can leave it up all year long. Below is an example:

Photo courtesy of Handprints Irish Gift Shop and Lamar Outdoor in Syracuse, NY

Your billboards can be placed in strategic locations to reach everyone coming into or going out of your market area. Your rep will show you a map of streets and highways in your area with board locations. From this map you can determine which boards will best serve your advertising needs. If you can't afford to put a board on every street leading to your business door, buy one or two billboards on a rotary program and have them periodically moved to the other appropriate sites.

Production

Outdoor's large physical characteristics—big, bold, and colorful—create a great visual impact on your audience. For this reason, you should carefully consider your creative efforts when deciding what your boards will look like. Many outdoor companies employ a creative director who will help you with content and design. If not, your rep will aid you in choosing a layout and deciding on the copy for your board(s).

Whether or not your outdoor company employs a designer to help you create a display that's memorable and motivating, your outdoor sales rep will have samples of award-winning designs to get you started. Make use of the exciting creative possibilities available with extensions, color (to attract attention and make your design stand out), and powerful text.

Make use of the exciting creative possibilities available with extensions, color (to attract attention and make your design stand out), and powerful text.

There are several methods of producing your design in paper, paint, and vinyl. One will surely fit your budget. As with other forms of advertising, if you are working with a limited budget, you may not opt for the most expensive form of production and decide to put the lion's share of the budget into the number of boards.

Paint and Vinyl Production

Vinyl is the most popular form of production for the big boards. Designs are computer-generated or painted onto a large sheet of vinyl, which is then slipped over the board like a large tablecloth and tightened in the back. Photo reproduction works well on vinyl: the finished product is more lifelike and three-deminsional than with painted boards or with paper. With paint you can have graphics in your design, but not photo reproduction.

If your boards will be up long term, you should know that paint stays beautiful for one or two years, while vinyl lasts for three or four years—both longer than paper, which usually needs changing every 45-60 days. Neon paint looks fantastic and really stands out, but tends to fade faster: you may get one or two years out of a vinyl with this type of paint, instead of three or four years. Your outdoor company will store your vinyl sheets for you if you intend to reuse them in the following months or even the following year.

Your outdoor company will take care of all of the production details for you. I go directly to the vinyl production companies to save the mark-up cost. If you produce your own design, you can too. You'll find them on the web: there are many companies you can find online with a Google or Yahoo search. Start with a keyword search for "outdoor billboard production."

Poster (Paper) Production

Poster paper production is for small boards (called posters). The designs are put on the billboards like wallpaper, in strips.

Your design can be generated from a photo negative or done with *flat tones,* which means you can still have illustrations, but they have a less realistic appearance (and they're less expensive to use) than a photograph. Your rep can show you samples of each. If you have co-op available to you from a supplier, ask if preprinted posters exist. A phone call can put them in your hands overnight and wipe out most of the production costs you would otherwise pay for. They will arrive fully printed, with the exception of a blank section at the bottom for your logo and address, which will be imprinted by your outdoor company.

The cost of poster paper production is determined by the number of colors you use and the numbers of posters you print. When using this kind of production, have a few extra posters printed at the beginning in case of vandalism or weather damage. It's less expensive to print a few extra posters with the first printing and then to have one or two more done at a later date. Remember that you can use vinyl on *any* size board—even posters.

Keep your boards simple and bright. Remember that people go by them quickly, so the artwork should be colorful and the message short—no more than eight to ten words plus your logo section. I know that when you're paying for advertising space you want to put as much information as you can on every board, but that is not the way outdoor works. There's only so much information people in a moving vehicle can absorb. You can present a forceful message with only a few words and a powerful graphic, like this board for a DWI campaign:

Keep your boards simple and bright. Remember that people go by them quickly, so the artwork should be colorful and the message short.

Extras

Solar rays are small foil-like discs that shake in the wind. Attach them at their centers to critical areas of your board to create a sparkle effect. Available in silver, gold, and many other colors, these light-throwers work very well in areas with a lot of sunshine. They can be used to make jewelry graphics glitter or the headlights of a car glow!

Teaser boards are intended to arouse curiosity and interest: a teaser board attracts your audience's attention and then keeps it until it provides the rest of the message. You can keep the first part of the design (the teaser section) up for the first half of the contract or just the first 10 days. Then add the second part of the message and your company logo.

Cut-outs or *extensions* give your overall design movement, extra dimension, and a larger, more exciting appearance. For a minimal charge per square foot (cost will vary depending on your geographic area), you can take your design off the edges of your board(s) in any or all of the four directions. The top third of a wine bottle can tower above the board. An elephant's trunk or the front end of a car can reach over one side of the board to create the illusion of movement. Again, your rep can show you samples of boards using cut-outs or extensions in their designs. The following example was provided by Warne/McKenna Advertising in Syracuse, NY:

For a minimal charge per square foot (cost will vary depending on your geographic area), you can take your design off the edges of your board(s) in any or all of the four directions.

Photo courtesy of Tarson Pools & Spas in North Syracuse, NY

Which Boards Do You Buy?

Drive by available boards and see if they are easily seen from the road. Are they clearly visible or are they obstructed by trees? Often, a board that cannot be seen in the summer because of trees can be clearly seen after the leaves have fallen. Does the board come up on you suddenly (maybe as you round a curve or pass by a tall structure) or is there a reasonable length of time on the approach (a long read)? When you consider locations, you should bypass a board that jumps out at you at the last minute.

Take note of the colors on other boards that catch your eye. Often there will be a series of two or three boards attached to each other in a grouping.

Which of the boards did you notice first? Perhaps the one closest to the road? Or the center board because its color and design made it stand out from the others?

When choosing between boards facing in opposite directions, choose those that people will see while driving *toward* your location(s), not when they're driving away from you, especially for "impulse products." The time to attract their attention is when they still have the opportunity to look for your store or office and it's convenient to stop because they happened to be in the neighborhood. If there are no boards in the "correct" position or if you're waiting for one to become available, use a board in close proximity but facing the opposite way until something better comes along. You don't want to give up the traffic in that area altogether while you're waiting. Boards for nonimpulse, higher-ticket items like cars, vacations, furniture, etc. can face any direction.

If you are renting lighted boards, drive by them occasionally at night to be sure the lights are functioning. They should remain lighted from sunset until midnight, but check with your representative for exact hours in your area.

Contracts

You will have the opportunity to work with your outdoor rep(s) to customize contracts for your particular budget. As with radio and television, you should discuss discounts for any long-term contracts, meaning 13 weeks or more. When committing yourself for a lengthy period, you should know that outdoor companies are among the toughest for allowing a contract cancellation.

When committing yourself for a lengthy period, you should know that outdoor companies are among the toughest for allowing a contract cancellation.

▶ Painted units are basically noncancelable. The upfront investment for the outdoor company is high and recaptured gradually over the life of the contract.

▶ Any long-term contract can pose a problem if you want to cancel halfway through. Before signing one, be sure you can afford it and look for a cancellation clause if you are concerned with finances.

▶ Look for an *automatic renewal clause* in your long-term contract—usually a contract that lasts for six months—and definitely on annuals! It means that, even though there is an end date on your contract, it will be automatically renewed unless you notify the company *in writing* of your desire not to renew. And you may have to give the written non-renewal as much as 90 days in advance of your contract end date.

161

The advantage of planning ahead is being able to secure the best board locations. But it would be wiser to take your chances on choosing from whatever boards are available closer to the time you want to advertise and buy one month at a time if you foresee any problem with financing. However, the risk you take buying this way is that someone else may reserve your board(s) and screw up your continuity.

> ▶ Buying outdoor is a lot easier than broadcast media, because it's more black and white. All you have to do is determine a good location and not worry about finding a specific station that will deliver your target audience.

> ▶ You probably have some idea about your desired location, so get out and drive around the area and see what billboards are available. Write down the names of the companies that own them. (That information is almost always printed somewhere.)

> ▶ Contact those companies and ask for rates for the specific locations you feel best suit your needs.

> ▶ Ask for daily traffic count information so that you know how many people drive by each day. (You can confirm these numbers by contacting your state Department of Transportation.)

> ▶ Don't be afraid to negotiate; outdoor advertising is like real estate—the seller always starts with a high asking price.

> ▶ Have a "take it or leave it" attitude when making an offer. If the outdoor company rep thinks you'll walk away from the deal, then he or she will be more likely to accept your offer.

Check with your local D.O.T. for road and highway closings or planned repair work that would cause traffic to be detoured around your billboard. Not many people do this, but you'd be surprised what a hassle it saves.

With all of the pluses outdoor has to offer (easy, equalizing, ever present, exciting), it is one of the first forms of advertising to check out. No other medium offers morning-to-night exposure, day after day, month after month.

What follows are some different types of outdoor signs available along with two worksheets for planning your outdoor advertising.

Bulletins. These large, illuminated boards deliver impact in size, placement, color, and lighting. They can measure 10.5 feet x 32 feet or 14 feet x 48 feet and larger. You'll find these along major highways.

30-sheet posters. These boards, placed along smaller roads and some high-

TIP: When the contracts on your boards expire, your outdoor company will probably leave your designs up until the locations are sold to someone else.

TIP: If something goes inexplicably wrong and you end up needing an extra poster, have your rep contact whoever produced the paper. There is almost always a "saved" copy printed and held just for these situations.

ways, deliver your message to residents and incoming travelers. These panels measure up to 12 feet x 26 feet.

8-sheet posters. These panels, measuring 6 feet x 12 feet, do the same job at a lower price and work well for 40 MPH and under—generally in the heart of most towns and cities.

Have your reps complete your Outdoor Billboard Worksheets when you are ready to consider outdoor advertising. Among other things, they will provide you with a list of available locations that would be appropriate for servicing your business. Because different board locations become available at various times throughout the year, plan as early as possible to ensure the best locations.

The completed worksheets will let you know at a glance when your contract starts and ends and, most importantly, when you need to notify the outdoor company to avoid an automatic renewal of your contract. They will also indicate production charges for your boards, that is, how much the paint, paper, or vinyl used on them will cost. The production fee is billed over and above the monthly rental charge.

The Outdoor Billboard Worksheet has a space for your rep to show you what your board will look like or for you to sketch out something for your rep to work from. This gives you an idea of the way your design fits within the height and width of your boards before you finalize a design and get into production. You will be provided with a proof before the final production is done and you will be asked to OK it. This absolves the production company from costly changes if the final results make you unhappy.

The Multiple Boards Worksheet lets you keep track of your boards—something that can get difficult to do if you have several up.

OUTDOOR BILLBOARD WORKSHEET
Have Your Reps Fill Out and Return This Sheet

Company Name _____

Rep's Name _____

Phone _____ Fax _____

E-mail _____

Board Size	Paper/ Paper/Vinyl	Location	Monthly Rent	Date Available
_____	_____	_____	$_____	_____
_____	_____	_____	$_____	_____
_____	_____	_____	$_____	_____
_____	_____	_____	$_____	_____
_____	_____	_____	$_____	_____
_____	_____	_____	$_____	_____
_____	_____	_____	$_____	_____
_____	_____	_____	$_____	_____

Production cost $_____ every # _____ days. Contract dates: _____ to _____

Does contract have an automatic renewal? Yes ___ No ___

Date of notification due: ___/___/___ In writing? Yes ___ No ___

Co-op being used? Yes ___ No ___ What brand? _____

Special instructions (color, etc.) _____

Sample Art Work

MULTIPLE BOARDS WORKSHEET					
Board #	Location	Up Date	Down Date	Production $	Monthly Rent
————	————	————	————	————	————
————	————	————	————	————	————
————	————	————	————	————	————
————	————	————	————	————	————
————	————	————	————	————	————
————	————	————	————	————	————
————	————	————	————	————	————
————	————	————	————	————	————
————	————	————	————	————	————
————	————	————	————	————	————
————	————	————	————	————	————
————	————	————	————	————	————
————	————	————	————	————	————
————	————	————	————	————	————
————	————	————	————	————	————
————	————	————	————	————	————
————	————	————	————	————	————
————	————	————	————	————	————

Chapter 19

Transit Advertising

WHERE DO YOU ADVERTISE WHEN YOU WANT TO REACH EVERY-body? Transit advertising—placement of print ads on buses and other vehicles and in bus shelters and train stations—is an important medium for reaching an audience of all ages, backgrounds, and incomes. You are not just addressing riders with these "moving billboards." You are reaching families and professionals in their vehicles, students shopping or right on campus, and tourists finding their way around town.

Why use transit advertising?

▶ You can't zap it.

▶ You can't ignore it.

▶ It can't be turned off like television.

▶ It reaches drivers and passengers no matter what radio stations they're listening to.

▶ The large, colorful, innovative designs demand attention.

▶ You have exclusivity in your space.

▶ It delivers a varied audience.

▶ It offers flexibility of ad size and location.

At one time, advertisers tended to shy away from *internal* transit advertising because of the perception of who the bus rider might be. Was the desired audience the person who could not afford a car? Today, concern for the environment and the popularity of programs such as Park-and-Ride have caused a wide range of business professionals, teachers, college students, and many other types of workers to leave their vehicles in mall parking lots and ride the bus to and from their jobs. It saves them the often high cost of parking and the wear-and-tear on their cars and provides them the opportunity to review material for a morning meeting, study, or just relax and gather their thoughts for the busy day ahead. The cards displayed inside the bus reach passengers who spend an average of 30-40 minutes on the bus ... and your ad is there for them to read the whole time.

Not only can you reach some very upscale customers on the inside of the bus, but you can also reach a large variety of people by advertising on the more traditional exterior signs. Available in various shapes and sizes, *exterior* bus signs display advertising messages to thousands of people in cars as well as pedestrians. Buses travel through cities and outlying suburban areas, to shopping malls, universities, business districts, amusement centers, supermarkets, theaters, and convention sites. Local customers as well as visitors to your area will be exposed to your large moving messages.

Not only can you reach some very upscale customers on the inside of the bus, but you can also reach a large variety of people by advertising on the more traditional exterior signs.

Types of Advertising

King and queen signs are located on the sides of transit vehicles. They are the largest of the signs and are attached to the bus with aluminum frames.

Tail signs are located on the rear of transit vehicles. If you've ever been stuck behind a bus at a traffic light or in a traffic jam, you know what the back of that bus says by the time you start moving again.

Interior cards are smaller and are seen only by the riders. They line the tops of the bus windows and include a sign located on the divider behind the bus driver (behind the driver sign). Some buses are assigned to school and college routes, so ask your transit company if you can put your signs in those particular buses to reach that younger audience.

You can buy all of the signs—inside and out—on one vehicle for tremendous impact. These "super-buses" or "mega-buses" can be fun buses to charter for special events.

In the last few years it has become more popular than ever in certain cities to "wrap" an entire bus with the theme of a company, a product, a museum, even camouflage wrap for an Army recruiting campaign. If it isn't all the rage in your city yet, it's coming—so don't be afraid to be the first to wrap a bus! These giant moving advertisements are impossible to miss and are a lot of fun to look at. A bus wrap is an expensive proposition and you will generally be required to sign a contract that will keep you paying rent on your bus for a minimum of one year. But if you have the budget and your company or product lends itself to the size and shape of a bus, you can get a lot of mileage (no pun intended) from this form of advertising. Discounts are available for buying multiple signs and for multiple-month contracts.

Now, if you don't want to wrap an entire bus, you can purchase one side and the back or one side and the front and share the bus with another advertiser. You can also purchase just the back or just the front of a bus.

Outdoor billboards and transit signs are very effective when used together, whether it is a full outdoor billboard or repeating your own store sign.

An example of a full wrap that's complemented by a series of designs displayed only on the back of other buses is provided by Bass Pro Shops in Auburn, New York. They have the following full design traveling through the Greater Syracuse, New York, market on just one bus, while using only their logo on the backs of multiple buses.

Photo courtesy of Bass Pro Shops

Outdoor billboards and transit signs are very effective when used together, whether it is a full outdoor billboard or repeating your own store sign. The combination keeps some of your signs anchored and some mobile for great coverage. A good example of this is the following bus/board designs provided by Obie Media in Eugene, Oregon:

168

Designs and Schedules

When considering your design, treat the signs as moving billboards. People won't have a chance to look at the message for a long period of time, so use bright colors to attract attention and simple ideas with just a few words for effective transit advertising.

When considering your design, treat the signs as moving billboards.

Whether you advertise in, on, or all over the bus, you can sometimes request that your bus travel on very specific routes or, if your message has broad audience appeal, on many routes so as to cover your maximum desired audience throughout your contract period. Your bus company will provide you with a complete list of routes.

If you plan on being a regular transit advertiser, speak to the director of marketing at your local bus company about placing an ad in the next batch of schedules printed. Schedules are usually updated annually, so if you decide to do this, use a generic ad that won't become outdated over that period of time.

Your Transit Worksheets will allow you to keep rates on hand for various sizes of signs and a complete record of what you purchase.

TRANSIT WORKSHEET #1

Have your transit rep fill out this worksheet for your general information. Go to Worksheet #2 when you are ready to use this form of advertising.

Company Name _____

Account Executive _____

Phone _____ Fax _____

E-mail _____

Monthly Rent

King Size $_____   Queen Size $_____   Traveling Displays $_____

Headlight Signs $_____   Tail Signs $_____   Driver Signs $_____

Bus Wraps $_____   Discounts Available _____

Production Cost

King Size $_____   Queen Size $_____   Traveling Displays $_____

Headlight Signs $_____   Tail Signs $_____   Driver Signs $_____

Bus Wraps $_____   Discounts Available _____

Side Panel Signs
King – 30" x 144"   Queen – 30" x 88"

Headlight Signs
21" x 40"

Tail Signs (bottom and top available)
21" x 70"

Traveling Displays
21" x 44"

Interior Signs
11" x 28"

Behind Driver Signs
14" x 19"

TRANSIT WORKSHEET #2

Have your transit rep fill out this worksheet when you are ready to advertise.

Company Name _____

Account Executive _____ •

Phone _____ Fax _____

E-mail _____

Dates of Schedule _____/_____/_____ to _____/_____/_____ # of Weeks _____

Total Number of Exterior Signs _____ Total Number of Interior Signs _____

# of King Size _____ # of Queen Size _____ # of Traveling Displays _____

# of Headlight Signs _____ # of Tail Signs _____ # of Driver Signs _____

# of Wraps _____ Discount _____

Production Cost $_____ Rent per Month $_____ Total Contract Cost $_____

Specific Routes _____
_____

❑ Please check here to request rotating bus(es) through all available routes.

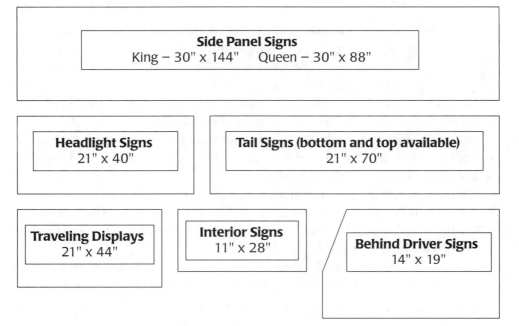

Side Panel Signs
King – 30" x 144"   Queen – 30" x 88"

Headlight Signs
21" x 40"

Tail Signs (bottom and top available)
21" x 70"

Traveling Displays
21" x 44"

Interior Signs
11" x 28"

Behind Driver Signs
14" x 19"

Chapter 20

Be Your Own Agency and Keep 15 Percent

O NE OF THE WAYS ADVERTISING AGENCIES MAKE MONEY IS BY EARN-
ing a 15 percent commission for placing paid advertising for
their clients. The percentage is based on the gross amount of
the budget. In other words, if a business has its agency place
$1,000 worth of advertising on a radio station, the client pays
the agency $1,000, but the agency pays the radio station only $850. This
commission does not really "cost" the business owner anything, because if
the bill is sent directly to him or her, and there is no agency involved, the cost
to the direct advertiser is still $1,000.

Most types of media recognize ad agencies and are reconciled to the fact
that they will be receiving 85 percent of the gross amounts billed, instead of
100 percent. It's not a bad trade-off, as agencies provide all forms of media
with a great deal of business.

If you are a large enough advertiser, you can declare yourself an *in-house*
agency and keep the 15 percent for yourself if you can meet a few requirements:

▶ You must have a decent budget. $40,000 to $50,000 per year would
probably be the minimum amount to establish yourself as an in-house
agency.

172

- ▶ You will write and deliver finished scripts for radio and television commercials.

- ▶ You will provide camera-ready copy to newspapers and magazines (or give specific instructions to your print reps as to how you want your ad to look).

- ▶ You design your own outdoor and transit signs or work with a designer to accomplish this.

- ▶ You deliver copy on time to all media outlets.

You will find that, while most forms of media recognize formal advertising agencies (and many in-house agencies) as a matter of routine, most newspapers do not recognize either kind. When you enter into a contract with any form of print advertising, check to see if the total is represented as a *gross* total, which includes a 15 percent agency commission, or as a *net* total, which does not include the 15 percent fee.

The small print on many contracts states that agencies are responsible for delivering finished radio and television spots to the station(s) two or three days in advance of schedules, rather than asking the reps to pick them up. But generally, reps provide pick-ups for agencies as a normal function of daily business. As a matter of fact, you can have copies of your TV or radio spot(s) left at the front desk at the station that produced them and notify the reps from other stations to pick them up there.

Small business owners do not normally have a large enough budget to worry about saving 15 percent at the risk of losing the talent and support that's always available from reps to direct advertisers. But for those direct advertisers who have a nice fat budget to back them up and the time to do the extra work or an employee designated to handle it for them, it's possible to save 15 percent of the advertising budget.

Over and above the 15 percent commission they earn on placed advertising, agencies charge an hourly fee to design print ads, outdoor billboards, transit ads, and direct mail pieces. They do media planning, media buying, market research, and a whole host of other things, including putting out fires that clients never hear about. Small local agencies may charge only $45 an hour for these services; large agencies can charge hundreds of dollars per hour.

These are all tasks you will have to take care of yourself, but interns can be very helpful with these chores. With interns on board who can perform all of the necessary duties on your behalf (and only with your final approval), you'd be well on your way to saving some big-time money. Often, it's money you can plow right back into your advertising budgets to give you more coverage! Interns can do the following:

- ▶ Write advertising copy and assist in overseeing production.
- ▶ Design outdoor billboards, direct mail, and print ads.
- ▶ Meet with printers to obtain quotes for brochures, letterhead, business cards, etc.
- ▶ Make sure props and/or talent gets to production on time.
- ▶ Set up and break down special event locations.
- ▶ Update your web site to reflect current ads.
- ▶ Keep co-op organized and meet submission deadlines.
- ▶ Do the legwork!

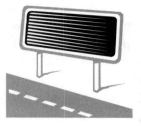

Chapter 21

Tracking

WE DON'T ALWAYS GET THE END RESULT THAT MAKES US HAPPY. Sometimes sales or promotions don't work out as we had hoped. Remember that the demographic numbers we use can only serve as a guide. There is no 100 percent guarantee that every advertising campaign will work. But if you have placed your advertising dollars properly, where your message reached your target market, the advertising will not be wasted. Even though your audience may not respond to the specifics of a certain campaign, it has heard your business name and your location and is getting familiar with what you do there—you've made another contact with "your people."

One of the hardest things to do is accurately track and analyze the results of your advertising. We do know that mail-back offers and coupons are tracked easily. But how do you track other kinds of advertising?

For businesses carrying a variety of inventories, it is possible to follow the sale of individual items or brands on different radio and television stations. For instance, a decorating outlet may advertise its wallpaper department on one particular radio station, advertise its furniture or carpet department on another radio station or on television, and advertise a paint sale in print or in a direct mail piece. The items showing a definite increase in business *during and immediately following the advertising* (memory will last only two weeks after the advertising stops) will tell the owner of that store which stations, print ads, or direct mail piece worked and which did not.

If you fill out a Tracking Results Worksheet for each campaign, you will see a pattern of how much money you spent, where you spent it, and what kind of results you experienced. If you advertise the same sale, product, or event in several forms of media in one campaign, you will know that the whole campaign worked or did not work, but you may not have a clear indication of which part worked the best. In this instance, don't worry too much. An overall success is always good news and, as you keep track of campaign after campaign, you will recognize how best to disperse your advertising funds.

The Annual Tracking Worksheet will tell you how much you actually spent during a 52-week period and where you spent it. Your advertising year does not have to start in January. It can start whenever you begin keeping track of your advertising on these worksheets, as long as you maintain the information for 52 consecutive weeks. Many businesses I have worked with have annual budgets that start in March or June. Your annual budget starts when you are ready to advertise or at least ready to keep track of your advertising dollars.

If you have taken the time to fill out the Tracking Results Worksheet for each campaign, add up the amounts spent on each medium and each vehicle within them (specific stations and publication, etc.). You will see if you placed the bulk of your advertising into one particular form of media or if you distributed the funds evenly into many forms.

Both tracking sheets are important to have with you when you negotiate future advertising rates. If you have kept accurate records, there will be no question as to how much you paid per spot or per column inch, what discount you received, or what you paid for production.

TIP: Plan your advertising. Last-minute advertising is like last-minute Christmas shopping. You end up paying too much money and you're not really happy with what you buy.

Remember to ask all of your reps to update the radio, television, print, direct mail, and outdoor advertising worksheets as rates officially change. But you should also do it because radio formats change, television programming changes, and, as the population in your market changes, the readership of various publications may change.

Once you get used to working from your worksheets, you will be able to make the *right* decisions quickly and save yourself enormous amounts of time and money to boot. You will spend less of your own personal time on advertising because your reps will be doing the work. And that's good—because you have a thousand other things to do every day!

The media worksheets in this book will provide critical standardized information free of "fluff" and irrelevant facts. Set up files with the tabs labeled in the following manner:

- ► Radio
- ► Television
- ► Print
- ► Direct Mail
- ► Outdoor
- ► Transit
- ► Tracking
- ► Extra Worksheets (includes Media Forms)

TRACKING RESULTS WORKSHEET

Date of campaign ____/____/____ to ____/____/____ Total budget $_____

Media used ❏ Radio ❏ Television ❏ Print ❏ Direct Mail ❏ Outdoor ❏ Transit

---

Radio stations and # of spots on each _____

_____ Production/talent cost $_____

Length of radio spots ❏ 10-second spots ❏ 60-second spots

❏ 30-second spots

TOTAL COST OF RADIO $_____

Television stations and # of spots on each _____

_____Production/talent cost $_____

Length of television spots ❏ 10-second spots ❏ 60 second spots

❏ 30-second spots

TOTAL COST OF TELEVISION $_____

Print/Publications used _____

Date of publication ___/___/___ Second date ___/___/___ Third date ___/___/___

Size of ad _____ Size of second ad _____ Size of third ad _____

TOTAL COST OF PRINT $_____

---

continued on next page

TRACKING RESULTS WORKSHEET (continued)

Number of direct mail pieces _____

Date mailed ___/___/___ Second mailing ___/___/___ Third mailing ___/___/___

Inserts

Publication used _____

Date ___/___/___ Second date ___/___/___

TOTAL COST OF DIRECT MAIL $_____

Outdoor billboards /company name _____

Number of boards _____ Size of boards _____

Location of boards _____

TOTAL COST OF OUTDOOR $_____

Transit/company name _____

Number of exterior signs _____ Number of interior signs _____

Production cost $_____ Rent per month $_____

Number of buses wrapped _____ Production cost $_____ Total rent $_____

TOTAL COST OF TRANSIT $_____

The campaign had ❑ no results ❑ some results ❑ good results ❑ great results

Notes: _____

_____

_____

Attach copies of radio and television scripts, print ads, and coupons to this sheet for future reference.

ANNUAL TRACKING WORKSHEET

Year ____/____/____ to ____/____/____ Total budget $_____

Media used: ❑ Radio ❑ Television ❑ Print ❑ Direct Mail ❑ Outdoor ❑ Transit

RADIO	TV
Station/Total Amount/Discount	**Station/Total Amount/Discount**
_____	_____
_____	_____
_____	_____
_____	_____
_____	_____
_____	_____
RADIO GRAND TOTAL $_____	**TV GRAND TOTAL** $_____

PRINT

Publication	Daily/Weekly	Discount %	Total Amount

PRINT GRAND TOTAL $_____

OUTDOOR BILLBOARDS		DIRECT MAIL	
Total Amount	**Rent & Production**	**Type (coupons/ brochures)**	**Total Amount**
OUTDOOR GRAND TOTAL $_____		**DIRECT MAIL GRAND TOTAL** $_____	

ANNUAL TRACKING WORKSHEET (continued)		
TRANSIT		
Total Amount	Total # of Signs (exterior & interior)	Total # of Wraps

TRANSIT GRAND TOTAL $_____

CO-OP	
Brands Used	Total Amount

TOTAL CO-OP DOLLARS CAPTURED $_____

The campaign had ❑ no results ❑ some results ❑ good results ❑ great results
Notes: _____
_____
_____

Attach copies of radio and television scripts, print ads, and coupons to this sheet for future reference.

Chapter 22

Conclusion

ADVERTISING SUCCESS DOESN'T HAPPEN OVERNIGHT. TIME IS required to establish your business name and build a brand. It's like pushing a ball uphill. You have to keep going because, if you stop pushing, the ball rolls back down the hill and you have to start all over. A snowball effect occurs with your continued advertising efforts, as each schedule builds upon whatever impact the previous schedule has made. The absolute worst thing to do is to start advertising and then disappear. You must make a commitment to advertising and have the strength to see it through.

Build, build, build.

Tom Attea, Managing Partner of Leap Frog Advertising in New York, NY (*www.leapfrogadv.com*), says:

Figure out the one best thing about your product or service. This is the foundation of your message. Decide on words and pictures that say it the best. This is the first floor of the building you will erect over time called your brand image. Then say it in the places that reach your target market to the extent that your budget allows. If you keep building on the same foundation, over the years you may have one of the highest buildings in your category; that is, your product will be more top of mind.

When you say the right thing, the right way, in the right places, advertising will do as much for you as it can. So you can put your head on your pillow at night knowing that the business you're doing is the business you *can* do in terms of how your advertising can help. You can spend your time taking care of the other aspects of your business. Advertising done this way is not a guessing game. It's a very skillful and powerful business tool.

Any form of advertising will work if used correctly. That's why you see ads for radio stations on bus signs, television ads in the newspaper, and commercials for your local transit company on the radio. They all use *each other*. This tells you emphatically that no one form of advertising can be expected to do it all for any business.

BBDO's Rob Cherof says:

Remember, no medium ever replaces another medium. They all complement each other. We still need newspapers, listen to the radio, and watch TV … and now we log onto the web as well. Figure out what you want each medium to do, then build them to do just that. Advertising is magical. As much as we try to make it into a science, somewhere along the line, we need to remember that how something feels is as important as whether or not it is technically right. All the great advertising feels right.

In the beginning, trial-and-error will have its place. Don't be afraid to adjust what you're doing when things don't seem to be working or to test different kinds of advertising to see what works best for you. You can't "try" advertising. Sticking your big toe in will never be enough. You have to *use* advertising.

Joseph Conrad, President and Strategic Director of Cactus Marketing Communications in Denver, CO (*www.sharpideas.com*), says,

Marketing is not magic, and success does not happen overnight. However, if you implement a consistent, cohesive, and integrated marketing program that simply communicates the essence of your business, the magic will happen in time because you create it.

Doing your part will make all the difference in how smooth or how riddled with grief your experience is. There are many responsibilities of a good advertiser:

Give plenty of notice. Give your media reps plenty of notice of upcoming advertising. You will be happier with your ads and the results they generate if you work ahead of time with your reps to give them a chance to think things through, look for upcoming special opportunities that correspond with your time requirements, and put extra effort into tying in copy and coordinating the layout and design of your print ads with your other media.

Be sensitive to deadlines.

- ▶ Radio is the form of media you can deal with the fastest in terms of producing commercials or starting a schedule within a day, as long as the station has the inventory available.

- ▶ Television is almost as fast, if inventory is available and if you already have a commercial produced.

- ▶ Print deadlines can vary from three to four days before publication for small papers to a week before publication with larger papers and sometimes 10 days to two weeks for special sections.

- ▶ Direct mail can have lead times of weeks to months ahead of mailing dates, depending on whether you're participating in a group mailing or going it alone.

- ▶ You'll need to have your outdoor and transit designs ready for the production houses two to three weeks ahead of posting time or, in the case of transit, wrapping. Here, especially with outdoor billboards, you buy specific dates that cannot easily be moved up or back a week or two, because others may already have contracted to rent the board you want.

Give accurate information before and after your advertising runs. One of the most counterproductive things you can do as an advertiser is to give false feedback to your media salespeople. When your reps ask you how the advertising worked, give totally accurate answers. Clients sometimes think if they indicate that the advertising did not work well, the rep will work harder the next time. In reality, if you tell a rep that your advertising did not work when it did, he or she will change what was done for the next schedule. Not only is this unfair to the rep who will waste precious time and energy trying to figure out what went wrong, but when the new schedule doesn't work, the rep will feel that he or she has let the client down and question his or her own ability. It's a bad scene all the way around. So if your advertising worked, please say so and give credit when credit is due. Of course, if it didn't work at all, be honest as well.

Check your invoices. When your invoices arrive at the end of each broadcast month, check them over thoroughly to be sure they correspond exactly with your original contracts. Make sure that the correct number of commercials or print ads ran and that they ran on the correct days and within the specified ranges of times. If you find any discrepancies, do not pay for the errant charges. Just subtract them from the total bill and let your rep know what you're doing and why. For instance, a typical radio contract might look like this:

	Monday	Tuesday	Wednesday	Thursday	Friday	Saturday
6A.M.-10A.M.	1X	1X	2X	2X	3X	2X
10A.M.-3P.M.	1X	1X	1X	1X	1X	1X
3P.M.-7P.M.		1X	1X	2X	2X	1X

This schedule represents 24 commercials to run in very specific dayparts over a six-day period. If the invoice comes in showing that one commercial ran at 5:25 A.M. (before the 6 A.M. start time) and one ran at 7:30 P.M. (after the 7 P.M. end time), you need not pay for those two commercials. If 23 of the spots ran correctly, but one ran on Sunday, which is not a contracted day, the Sunday spot should be deducted from the bill. This is something you need to do with every invoice.

Sometimes spots do get moved for a variety of reasons. If the traffic department of a radio or television station needs to move one of your spots, your rep will usually be told and, in turn, the rep will alert you to see what you want to do. Move the spot? Cancel the spot? It's up to you. However, now and then something will happen to a schedule without the rep's knowledge. You are the final examiner of the paperwork and, since it's your money, don't overlook the step.

If your print ad runs with the wrong colors or in the wrong layout or it deviates from your instructions, ask for a make-good. If one can't be given in time for your sale or event, get the charge eliminated. Print reps might ask you to consider whether the ad had any value at all, even though it wasn't 100 percent the way you wanted it. This is an attempt to get you to pay a percent of the bill rather than not pay at all.

Ask him or her this question: "If the guests at your daughter's wedding were supposed to be fed prime rib and shrimp at the reception, but were fed baked chicken and potato salad instead, would you pay for the meal?" The caterer could argue that there was some value to the meal because the wedding guests ate it—it served a purpose. I can guarantee you that the rep would not pay for the meal. A reception menu is chosen specifically to match the atmosphere of the wedding and the character of the family and as a thank-you to the guests who attended and brought gifts. Chicken would not fill the bill when prime rib was ordered.

The look of your print ad—the colors, the design, the copy, etc.—must create a feeling, a look, and provide an impression of your company. You put a lot of thought, work, and money into getting it just right and running it at just the right time. Make sure it's what you intended. Don't pay for chicken when you ordered prime rib.

Pay your invoices on time. Everyone in the business knows who pays on time and who doesn't. Monthly collection meetings are held within every media sales department to discuss clients who are behind in their payments. And all reps have friends within the business. They know who pays within 30 days and who is way out there. You won't be able to negotiate your next advertising schedule from a position of strength and you don't want to go back to the days of being asked to pay cash in advance—especially after you've worked hard to reach the point where you can call in a schedule and have it happily taken over the phone.

Offer gift certificates for product or services. Gift certificates are a great way to increase your business, especially during the holidays. Instead of buying stock certificates off the shelf, create your own so they're more difficult to duplicate.

- ▶ Use specialty paper.
- ▶ Make one or two identifying marks on the certificates.
- ▶ Number the certificates.
- ▶ Fill them out completely at the time of purchase with carbon paper or photocopy each one.
- ▶ Include an end date.

Employ one or more of these suggestions to verify the authenticity of your gift certificates when they are brought to you for redemption. Gift certificates allow you to keep more inventory in the store during peak shopping times. Also, some of the certificates you sell will never be redeemed.

Diplomacy under fire. Dealing with the public is not easy. There are always those people who will argue about what your ads say, challenge your return policy, complain about your inventory, and try to wheedle something extra out of you at every turn. It comes with the territory and, yes, it can make you want to tear your hair out. But take it in stride and do what you can to placate the worst of the lot.

When your best attempts fail to satisfy those really tough ones, send them to your largest competitor—it'll make you feel better!

Ducking friendly fire. I don't need a crystal ball to know that your accountant will knock on your door (each and every year), say that you spend too much money on advertising, and recommend you reduce it to improve the bottom line. Tell him or her about that wink in the dark and ask for suggestions on how you can otherwise motivate customers to line up in front of your cash register. Hopefully you can make the point that without advertising you *are* winking in the dark!

Plan your party! Advertising is your way of inviting the public to your business door. Just as you would not invite all of humanity to a party, you will work from a specific "guest list" when preparing to send out your invitations. Stick to the people on that guest list and deliver invitations to them that they will not be able to resist. Remember that other businesses are inviting the same crowd to their parties! So be sure your invitation is bigger, better, louder, and more alluring than the others they receive. Make it a great party for them and invite them back consistently.

I would like to wish you all the very best of luck with your business and I hope that this book will play a role in saving you some time and money along the way.

Glossary

Adjacency. A commercial placed right next to a special feature such as weather, news, sports, or traffic reports.

Affidavit. Notarized invoices showing specific days and times commercials ran. All co-op invoices and scripts must be notarized for authorization.

Afternoon Drive. The 3-7 P.M. section of a radio day or daypart.

Announcement. Commercial message of varying lengths on radio or television.

Annual Discount. Rate discount applied to contracts of 52 continuous week duration.

Arbitron. Radio rating service measuring listening/viewing audiences.

Audience Composition. Demographic makeup of a group of people represented in audience grouped by age and gender.

Automatic Renewal. A clause sometimes found in outdoor advertising contracts indicating the need to cancel contracts in writing 90 days in advance to avoid the automatic renewal of the contract.

Behind the Driver Sign. An advertising space on busses located on the divider behind the driver.

Billboard (Outdoor). Painted, printed, or poster advertising boards along roads and highways.

Billboard (Radio). An ID announcement of a program or feature sponsor.

Branding. The process of building a business name and reputation.

Brochure. Printed promotional piece available in many sizes.

Cable. Television signals transmitted by wire or cable, instead of through the air. Cable television provides programming from more and distant stations for a monthly fee.

Cancellation Date. A specific, published date for canceling an advertising contract.

Circulation (Outdoor). Number of people who drive by a given board location with a 24-hour period.

Circulation (Print). Number of copies sold or delivered.

Column Inch. A newspaper measurement of the smallest possible ad—one column wide by one inch long.

Co-op Advertising. The sharing of the cost of advertising between an advertiser and a manufacturer.

Copy. The written script for radio or television spots or the word section of a print ad.

Coupon(ing). Distribution of coupons through the mail, print, or in-store promotion.

Coverage Map. Diagram showing a medium's geographical audience potential.

Daypart. A specific segment of a broadcast day.

Demographics. Segments of population grouped by age and gender.

Direct Mail. Print pieces sent through the mail to consumers.

Domain Registration. Reserving the name (URL) of your web site.

Donut. A cost-effective form of a television or radio spot. The beginning and the end are produced with generic information, leaving the center of the spot blank, to allow insertion of different information.

Drive Time. Morning and afternoon radio dayparts (5:30-10 A.M. and 3-7 P.M.).

Dub. A copy of a radio or television commercial.

Exclusivity. Advertising at a given period of time, free from competing ads.

Fixed Rate. Cost of spots running at the same time every day.

Flat Rate. Advertising rate before discounts.

Frequency. Average number of times a person is exposed to a commercial message.

Frequency Discount. Discount given for reaching a specific number of commercials of print, radio, television, or outdoor ads per week, month, or year.

Flight. A short radio or television schedule.

Font. Style of lettering.

Gross Amount. Includes a 15-percent commission fee. If you are an in-house agency, deduct 15-percent before paying your bill.

In-House Agency. The term given to an advertiser who independently plans and places media schedules, provides his or her own produced commercials and print ads, and receives a 15-percent commission for doing so.

Insert. A printed piece delivered to consumers inside of a daily or weekly newspaper.

King Sign. Advertising attached to the sides of transit vehicles with aluminum frames. See also *queen sign*.

Maintenance Advertising. See *strategic advertising*.

Make-Good. A commercial run as a replacement for one missed or pre-exempted from a regular schedule on radio, on television, or in print.

Net Amount. Does not include a 15-percent agency fee. You must pay amount shown.

Nielsen. A.C. Nielsen Company, a national television rating service.

Out-of-Home Advertising. Ads on and in buses, transit shelters and stations, along roads, around malls, in airports—anywhere that people go.

Poster. The smallest outdoor billboards available.

Primary Audience. A station's largest demographic segment of viewers or listeners.

Promotion. A heightened form of advertising including special extra features.

PSA. Public Service Announcement.

Pulsing. Advertising technique of scheduling alternating periods of advertising and periods without advertising. Example: one week on, one week off.

Queen Sign. Advertising attached to the sides of transit vehicles with aluminum frames. See also *king sign*.

Rate Card. A published list of rates, deadlines, and cancellation specifications for all media.

Rating. The audience shown as a percent of the total population.

Reach. The number of different persons or households exposed to a commercial message.

Remnant Space. Radio, television, or print space sold at reduced rates.

Remote. Broadcasting a radio or television show from an outside location.

Roadblocking. Buying the same time slot on all television networks at the same time with the intent of catching everyone watching TV at that time. Most often done with news.

Rotary Program. Rotating outdoor billboards between or among locations over a period of time.

Shared Advertising. An advertising campaign featuring the sharing of commercial production and cost by two or more advertisers.

Shopper. A local, weekly newspaper usually delivered to homes at no cost.

Showing. A group of outdoor billboards up at one time in various locations.

Sponsorship. The purchase by one advertiser of a specific station feature such as weather, sports, news, or traffic reports.

Spot. One commercial on radio or television.

Strategic Advertising. Running a small schedule over a long period of time. Also called *maintenance advertising*.

Sweeps. Both Arbitron and Nielsen survey all television local markets four times per year (November, February, May, and July).

SWOT Analysis. Strengths, weaknesses, opportunities, and threats. A review of these essential considerations is used to guide advertising.

Tabloid. A smaller than standard-sized newspaper or special newspaper section.

Tactical Advertising. Running a large amount of commercials in a short period of time.

Tail Signs. Advertising on the rear of transit vehicles.

TAP. See *total audience plan.*

Target Audience. A specific group of people defined by age and gender by an advertiser.

Tear Sheet. An actual page containing the advertising being invoiced as proof of publication.

Total Audience Plan (TAP). A radio schedule made up of all dayparts at a reasonable rate.

Transit Advertising. Placement of print ads on buses and other vehicles and in bus shelters and train stations.

Unit. One radio or television spot.

Vehicle. A specific station or publication within a general media classification. Can also refer to outdoor billboards and transit. Any form of advertising.

Volume Discount. A rate discount given for running a specific (large) number of radio, television, or print ads within a given contract.

Worksheets

THIS SECTION OF THE BOOK INCLUDES COPIES OF ALL OF THE WORK-sheets and forms in this book so that you can duplicate and use them. Establishing structure in your advertising program is critical to taking control of your expenditures. Organize your completed paperwork: it will save you time and help keep your budget under control.

Make extra copies right off the bat of the worksheets for radio, television, print, direct mail, outdoor, and transit. When a rep calls on you, you'll have them to hand out. Every rep who calls on you should leave with a worksheet.

Whether you use a binder or folders to keep them straight, stash them where you can get to them quickly and, if you can manage it, keep them in the same location as the copies of your radio and television spots and other advertising materials.

CUSTOMER INFORMATION WORKSHEET

Dates: From _____ to _____

ZIP Codes	Gender	Age (estimate)
_____	_____	_____
_____	_____	_____
_____	_____	_____
_____	_____	_____
_____	_____	_____
_____	_____	_____
_____	_____	_____
_____	_____	_____
_____	_____	_____
_____	_____	_____
_____	_____	_____
_____	_____	_____
_____	_____	_____
_____	_____	_____
_____	_____	_____
_____	_____	_____
_____	_____	_____
_____	_____	_____
_____	_____	_____
_____	_____	_____
_____	_____	_____
_____	_____	_____
_____	_____	_____
_____	_____	_____
_____	_____	_____

TOTALS

_____	Females _____	_____
_____		_____
_____	Males _____	_____
_____		

SWOT WORKSHEET	
Strengths	**Weaknesses**
What efforts will you make to keep them? _____ _____ _____	What efforts will you make to strengthen them? _____ _____ _____
Opportunities	**Threats**
How will you take advantage of them? _____ _____ _____	How will you overcome them? _____ _____ _____

Radio Demographic Rankings
Worksheet #1

Station: _____Date: _____

Circle the same choices below from Groups A and B as you did in Chapter 5. Have your radio rep(s) fill out *only the sections that match those selections*. This worksheet, when completed by your reps, will indicate how the top four stations reaching your desired audience(s) compare with each other. The information will be excerpted from research companies such as Arbitron and Nielsen and represents the most accurate data available.

GROUP A (age)
18-34
18-49
25-54
45+

GROUP B (gender)
Female
Male
Adults (both male and female)

Source _____

Note to Rep: Please use average persons (00)

Market: Total Survey Area

Monday-Friday 5:30 A.M.-7 P.M.

Women 18-34	Men 18-34	Adults 18-34
1. _____	_____	_____
2. _____	_____	_____
3. _____	_____	_____
4. _____	_____	_____

Women 18-49	Men 18-49	Adults 18-49
1. _____	_____	_____
2. _____	_____	_____
3. _____	_____	_____
4. _____	_____	_____

Women 25-54	Men 25-54	Adults 25-54
1. _____	_____	_____
2. _____	_____	_____
3. _____	_____	_____
4. _____	_____	_____

Continued on next page

	Women 45+	Men 45+	Adults 45+
1.	_____	_____	_____
2.	_____	_____	_____
3.	_____	_____	_____
4.	_____	_____	_____

Saturday-Sunday 9 A.M.-Midnight

	Women 18-34	Men 18-34	Adults 18-34
1.	_____	_____	_____
2.	_____	_____	_____
3.	_____	_____	_____
4.	_____	_____	_____

	Women 18-49	Men 18-49	Adults 18-49
1.	_____	_____	_____
2.	_____	_____	_____
3.	_____	_____	_____
4.	_____	_____	_____

	Women 25-54	Men 25-54	Adults 25-54
1.	_____	_____	_____
2.	_____	_____	_____
3.	_____	_____	_____
4.	_____	_____	_____

	Women 45+	Men 45+	Adults 45+
1.	_____	_____	_____
2.	_____	_____	_____
3.	_____	_____	_____
4.	_____	_____	_____

Notes:

_____

_____

_____

_____

_____

_____

Submitted by: _____ _____ _____

Name of Salesperson   Station   Date

Phone: _____ Fax: _____ E-mail: _____

RADIO WORKSHEET #2
Have Your Reps Fill Out and Return This Sheet

Radio Station Information

Call Letters _____ Dial Position _____

Rep's Name _____

Phone # _____ E-mail _____

Format _____

Demographic Strength

Sales Rep: Circle the choices from Groups A and B that best describe your station's primary strength.

Group A (age)	Group B (gender)
18-34	Female
18-49	Male
25-54	Adults
45+	

Cost per week based on frequency of 12X, 18X, 24X, Monday-Friday 5:30A-Midnight

(:60 sec)　12X per week $_____ (3X 5:30a-10a, 3X 10a-3p, 3X 3p-7p, 3X 7p-mid)

18X per week $_____ (4X 5:30a-10a, 5X 10a-3p, 5X 3p-7p, 4X 7p-mid)

24X per week $_____ (6X 5:30a-10a, 6X 10a-3p, 6X 3p-7p, 6X 7p-mid)

Cost per week based on weekends Friday-Sunday 10A-10P

(:60 sec)　12X per week $_____ (4X 10a-3p, 4X 3p-7p, 4X 7p-10p)

18X per week $_____ (6X 10a-3p, 6X 3p-7p, 6X 7p-10p)

24X per week $_____ (8X 10a-3p, 8X 3p-7p, 8X 7p-10p)

Sponsorships Available (based on :60 second spots)

Type of Sponsorship	Times per Week	Price per Week	Audience
News *Billboards are/are not included*	2X (T, Th) 3X (M, W, F) 5X (M-F)	$_____ $_____ $_____	_____ (age) _____ (sex)
Weather *Billboards are/are not included*	2X (T, Th) 3X (M, W, F) 5X (M-F)	$_____ $_____ $_____	_____ (age) _____ (sex)
Sports *Billboards are/are not included*	2X (T, Th) 3X (M, W, F) 5X (M-F)	$_____ $_____ $_____	_____ (age) _____ (sex)
Air Traffic *Billboards are/are not included*	2X (T, Th) 3X (M, W, F) 5X (M-F)	$_____ $_____ $_____	_____ (age) _____ (sex)

RADIO WORKSHEET #2
Have Your Reps Fill Out and Return This Sheet

Sample General Weekday Schedules

12X	M	T	W	Th	F
5:30-10A	X		X		X
10-3P		X	X	X	
3-7P	X		X		X
7-10P		X	X	X	

Cost $_____

18X	M	T	W	Th	F
5:30-10A	X		X	X	X
10-3P	X	X	X	X	X
3-7P	X	X	X	X	X
7-10P	X	X	X	X	

Cost $_____

24X	M	T	W	Th	F
5:30-10A	XX	X	X	X	X
10-3P	X	X	XX	X	X
3-7P	X	XX	X	X	X
7-10P	X	X	X	XX	X

Cost $_____

Sample Schedules for Early-Mid Week Business

12X	M	T	W
5:30-10A	X	X	X
10-3P	XX	X	X
3-7P	X	XX	X
7-10P	X	X	

Cost $_____

18X	M	T	W
5:30-10A	XX	X	XX
10-3P	XX	XX	XX
3-7P	XX	X	
7-10P	XX	XX	

Cost $_____

24X	M	T	W
5:30-10A	XXX	XX	XX
10-3P	XX	XXX	XX
3-7P	XXX	XX	
7-10P	XX	XXX	

Cost $_____

Sample Schedules for Late Week and Weekend Business

12X	M	T	W	Th	F	Sa
5:30-10A			X	X	X	
10-3P			X	X		X
3-7P			X		X	X
7-10P			X	X		

Cost $_____

18X	M	T	W	Th	F	Sa
5:30-10A				X	X	XX
10-3P				XX	X	XX
3-7P				X	XX	XX
7-10P				X	XX	X

Cost $_____

24X	M	T	W	Th	F	Sa
5:30-10A				X	XX	XX	X
10-3P				X	X	XX	XX
3-7P				X	XX	XX	X
7-10P				X	XX	XX	X

Cost $_____

Sample Schedules for Weekend Business

12X	F	Sa	Su
5:30-10A			
10-3P		XX	XX
3-7P	XX	XX	
7-10P	XX	XX	

Cost $_____

18X	F	Sa	Su
5:30-10A			
10-3P		XXX	XXX
3-7P	XXX	XXX	
7-10P	XXX	XXX	

Cost $_____

24X	F	Sa	Su
5:30-10A			
10-3P		XXXX	XXXX
3-7P	XXXX	XXXX	
7-10P	XXXX	XXXX	

Cost $_____

If you are not open Sunday or your event ends on Saturday, move Sunday spots back into Friday and Saturday. Or feel free to ask for a 10 P.M. cutoff time on any schedule.

30-Second Radio Copy Form

Using an 11-point font, use this eight-line sheet for a standard 30-second script. Do not use any abbreviations, numerals, or substitutions, such as "&" for "and." All words take the same amount of time to *say* no matter how you write them. So, for an accurately timed script, spell out all words. Use all caps for easier reading. (Recreate this form on a letter-size page for the eight-line rule to work.)

1.

2.

3.

4.

5.

6.

7.

8.

Client: _____

Title of Spot: _____

Runs ____/____/____ to ____/____/____

Special instructions: _____

_____

_____

_____

_____

_____

60-Second Radio Copy Form

Use this type of sheet for a standard 60-second script.

1.
2.
3.
4.
5.
6.
7.
8.
9.
10.
11.
12.
13.
14.
15.
16.

Client: _____

Title of Spot: _____

Runs ____/____/____ to ____/____/____

Special instructions: _____

_____

_____

_____

_____

_____

TELEVISION WORKSHEET
Have Your Reps Fill Out and Return This Sheet

Note to Account Executive: Include only programs geared to demographics noted below:

Station _____ Network _____ Cable _____

Dial Position _____

Rep's Name _____

Phone # _____ E-mail _____

Account _____

Business Owner: Circle choices from groups A and B that correspond with those you chose in Define Your Market

Group A (age)	Group B (gender)
18-34	Female
18-49	Male
25-54	Adults (both male and female)
45+	

Weekdays

Time Period	Program	Price Per :30	Per :10/:15

Weekends

Time Period	Program	Price Per :30	Per :10/:15

PRINT WORKSHEET
Have Your Reps Fill Out and Return This Sheet

Publication: _____

Rep's Name: _____

Phone: _____

E-Mail: _____

Publication is: ❏ Daily   ❏ Weekly   ❏ Other

Ad Size	Price	Day Ad Will Run
Full Page	$_____	_____
1/2 Page	$_____	_____
1/4 Page	$_____	_____
1/8 Page	$_____	_____
Other	$_____	_____

Special Sections Geared to This Business

Summer	Fall	Winter	Spring
_____	_____	_____	_____
_____	_____	_____	_____
_____	_____	_____	_____
_____	_____	_____	_____
_____	_____	_____	_____
_____	_____	_____	_____
_____	_____	_____	_____
_____	_____	_____	_____
_____	_____	_____	_____

Contract rate per column inch: $_____

Contract start date: _____/_____/_____   End date: _____/_____/_____

DIRECT MAIL WORKSHEET

Company Name _____ Sales Rep _____

Address _____ Phone _____

Fax _____ E-mail _____

❏ Group Mailing ❏ Individual Mailing ❏ Inserts

❏ Single-Sided ❏ Double-Sided ❏ Folded

Number of pieces _____ Size of piece _____

How many colors/which colors? _____

If inserts, name of publication _____ Publication date _____

Insertion cost per thousand $_____

Postage cost if mailing $_____ Mailing date _____

ZIP codes/areas covered _____

Deadline for final design and copy _____/_____/_____

Date of proof _____/_____/_____ Changes made _____

_____

_____

Final approval date _____/_____/_____

Total cost (including postage or insertion charge, tax, etc.) $_____

Title of this direct mail campaign _____

Offer or sale _____

End date on offer _____/_____/_____

OUTDOOR BILLBOARD WORKSHEET
Have Your Reps Fill Out and Return This Sheet

Company Name _____

Rep's Name _____

Phone _____ Fax _____

E-mail _____

Board Size	Paint/ Paper/Vinyl	Location	Monthly Rent	Date Available
_____	_____	_____	$_____	_____
_____	_____	_____	$_____	_____
_____	_____	_____	$_____	_____
_____	_____	_____	$_____	_____
_____	_____	_____	$_____	_____
_____	_____	_____	$_____	_____
_____	_____	_____	$_____	_____
_____	_____	_____	$_____	_____

Production cost $_____ every # _____ days. Contract dates: _____ to _____

Does contract have an automatic renewal? Yes ___ No ___

Date of notification due: ____/____/____ In writing? Yes ___ No ___

Co-op being used? Yes ___ No ___ What brand? _____

Special instructions (color, etc.) _____

Sample Art Work

MULTIPLE BOARDS WORKSHEET					
Board #	Location	Up Date	Down Date	Production $	Monthly Rent

TRANSIT WORKSHEET #1

Have your transit rep fill out this worksheet for your general information. Go to Worksheet #2 when you are ready to use this form of advertising.

Company Name _____

Account Executive _____

Phone _____ Fax _____

E-mail _____

Monthly Rent

King Size $_____   Queen Size $_____   Traveling Displays $_____

Headlight Signs $_____   Tail Signs $_____   Driver Signs $_____

Bus Wraps $_____   Discounts Available _____

Production Cost

King Size $_____   Queen Size $_____   Traveling Displays $_____

Headlight Signs $_____   Tail Signs $_____   Driver Signs $_____

Bus Wraps $_____   Discounts Available _____

Side Panel Signs
King – 30" x 144"   Queen – 30" x 88"

Headlight Signs
21" x 40"

Tail Signs (bottom and top available)
21" x 70"

Traveling Displays
21" x 44"

Interior Signs
11" x 28"

Behind Driver Signs
14" x 19"

TRANSIT WORKSHEET #2

Have your transit rep fill out this worksheet when you are ready to advertise.

Company Name _____

Account Executive _____

Phone _____ Fax _____

E-mail _____

Dates of Schedule _____/_____/_____ to _____/_____/_____ # of Weeks _____

Total Number of Exterior Signs _____ Total Number of Interior Signs _____

# of King Size _____ # of Queen Size _____ # of Traveling Displays _____

# of Headlight Signs _____ # of Tail signs _____ # of Driver Signs _____

# of Wraps _____ Discount _____

Production Cost $_____ Rent per Month $_____ Total Contract Cost $_____

Specific Routes _____

_____

❏ Please check here to request rotating bus(es) through all available routes.

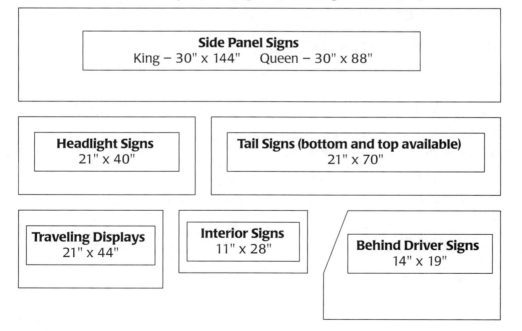

Side Panel Signs
King – 30" x 144"   Queen – 30" x 88"

Headlight Signs
21" x 40"

Tail Signs (bottom and top available)
21" x 70"

Traveling Displays
21" x 44"

Interior Signs
11" x 28"

Behind Driver Signs
14" x 19"

TRACKING RESULTS WORKSHEET

Date of campaign ____/____/____ to ____/____/____ Total budget $_____

Media used: ❏ Radio ❏ Television ❏ Print ❏ Direct Mail ❏ Outdoor ❏ Transit

Radio stations and # of spots on each _____

_____ Production/talent cost $_____

Length of radio spots   ❏ 60-second spots   ❏ 30-second spots

TOTAL COST OF RADIO $_____ (include production)

Television stations and # of spots on each _____

_____Production/talent cost $_____

Length of television spots   ❏ 10-second spots   ❏ 60-second spots

❏ 30-second spots

TOTAL COST OF TELEVISION $_____ (include production)

Print/Publication(s) used _____

Date of Publication ___/___/___ Second date ___/___/___ Third date ___/___/___

Size of ad _____ Size of second ad _____ Size of third ad _____

TOTAL COST OF PRINT $_____ (include production)

Number of direct mail pieces _____

Date mailed ___/___/___ Second mailing ___/___/___ Third mailing ___/___/____

Inserts

Publication used _____

Date ___/___/___ Second date ___/___/___

TOTAL COST OF DIRECT MAIL $_____ (include production)

Outdoor billboards/company name _____

Number of boards _____ Size of boards _____

Location of boards _____

TOTAL COST OF OUTDOOR $_____ (include production)

continued on next page

TRACKING RESULTS WORKSHEET

Transit/company name _____

Number of exterior signs _____ Number of interior signs _____

Production cost $_____ Rent per month $_____

Number of buses wrapped _____ Production cost $_____ Total rent $_____

TOTAL COST OF TRANSIT $_____ (include production)

The campaign had ❏ no results ❏ some results ❏ good results ❏ great results

Notes: _____

_____

_____

Attach copies of radio and television scripts, print ads, and coupons to this sheet for future reference.

ANNUAL TRACKING WORKSHEET

Year ____/____/____ to ____/____/____ Total budget $_____

Media used: ❏ Radio ❏ Television ❏ Print ❏ Direct Mail ❏ Outdoor ❏ Transit

RADIO	TV
Station/Total Amount/Discount	**Station/Total Amount/Discount**
_____	_____
_____	_____
_____	_____
_____	_____
_____	_____
_____	_____
RADIO GRAND TOTAL $_____	**TV GRAND TOTAL** $_____

PRINT			
Publication	**Daily/Weekly**	**Discount %**	**Total Amount**

PRINT GRAND TOTAL $_____

OUTDOOR BILLBOARDS		DIRECT MAIL	
Total Amount	**Rent & Production**	**Type (coupons/ brochures)**	**Total Amount**
OUTDOOR GRAND TOTAL $_____		**DIRECT MAIL GRAND TOTAL** $_____	

Coninued on next page

Annual Tracking Worksheet		
TRANSIT		
Total Amount	**Total # of Signs (exterior & interior)**	**Total # of Wraps**
_____	_____	_____
_____	_____	_____
_____	_____	_____

TRANSIT GRAND TOTAL $_____

CO-OP	
Brands Used	**Total Amount**
_____	_____
_____	_____

TOTAL CO-OP DOLLARS CAPTURED $_____

Attach copies of radio and television scripts, print ads, and coupons to this sheet for future reference.

Index

The following pages contain material from *Entrepreneur* **Media's**
Accounting and Finance for Small Business Made Easy **by**
Robert Low. **Available at all fine bookstores nationwide**
and online retailers.
ISBN: 1-932531-17-3
$19.95

Chapter 1

Understanding Financial Management

> Is it not as impossible in trade that a merchant should be as prosperous without being a thorough-pac'd accountant … as that a mariner should conduct a ship to all parts of the globe without a skill in navigation?
> —Anonymous London Merchant, circa 1700

A STORY IS TOLD ABOUT A BALLOONIST WHO GETS LOST AND IS forced to make an emergency landing in an open field. The balloonist flags down a passerby and asks him, "Where am I?"

"You are in a balloon basket in the middle of a field" is the reply.

"You must be an accountant," says the balloonist. "The information you just gave me is perfectly accurate and of absolutely no use."

"And you," replies the passerby, "must be a CEO [chief executive officer]. You are operating a craft over which you have no control and want me to tell you where you are going."[1]

This story depicts the gap that can exist between nonfinancial managers and accountants. Accountants often focus on providing accurate numbers, which may not be relevant or timely. Many business owners and managers, though, steer their businesses using a seat-of-the pants style and could benefit from financial know-how and controls.

Effective accounting, planning, and control often mean the difference between success and failure for smaller companies.

As a small business owner or manager, you will want strong communication and support between you and your financial staff. Effective accounting, planning, and control often mean the difference between success and failure for smaller companies. Yet, many smaller business owners, although skilled providers of a service or product, often operate with little background in financial management. This can contribute to:

▶ Shortsighted management decisions

▶ Misallocation of resources

▶ Failure to anticipate crises

Whether you are the owner of a smaller business or a manager in a larger corporation or division, you can avoid these costly mistakes if your company has an accounting and finance department that plays a dynamic and diversified role in management support. To get there, nonfinancial managers need enough interest and background to work with their key finance and accounting people. Conversely, the financial managers must appreciate the aspects of accounting and controllership beyond simply processing transactions and producing financial statements. These include management accounting, planning, asset management, and internal controls, activities that support internal management and decision making.

The number and types of financial advisors and staff members you employ will vary depending on the needs of your business. Your accounting department may consist of only a bookkeeper, an accountant, or both. On the other hand, you may employ a chief financial officer (CFO) or controller, plus an entire support staff. You will likely rely on an outside certified public accountant for tax work and, perhaps, financial statement audits or more. While the next chapter goes into greater detail about the types of financial and accounting players, the main distinctions among the job titles you might encounter are as follows:

▶ **Bookkeepers and accountants** usually do the mechanical work of daily transactions and the compiling of financial statements.

▶ **Controllers** oversee accounting, but also have operating responsibilities, including interpreting financial information, controlling expenses and cash flow, planning, and implementing internal controls. See Chapter 6 for more information about the controller's role.

▶ **CFOs** usually supervise the controller, but also have responsibility for the financing, treasury, and administrative activities of a company.

▶ **CPA firms** are outside advisors who specialize in tax preparation and auditing.

No matter how small or large your business is, and no matter how many and what kind of financial advisors you employ, your leadership and direction of your accounting department are the important factors for having the information you need to become a hands-on manager.

This introductory chapter provides you with an overview of the financial management issues you need to be aware of to successfully operate your business. It discusses why it is critical for business owners and financial advisors to work well together and why, in practice, they don't.

Financial Information Gap

In many, if not most companies today, a wide gap exists between the needs of business owners and managers for financial information, systems, and control and what is being provided by their internal financial managers and CPAs. This gap creates a serious vulnerability, particularly for smaller businesses, which operate with less margin for error than large corporations.

Several authors have blamed 60-80% of business failures on financial problems, including poor record keeping and factors linked to cash flow.

While the risk may not be easily quantifiable, it seems hard to overstate. Several authors have blamed 60-80% of business failures on financial problems, including poor record-keeping and factors linked to cash flow.[2] On the positive side, a study has established the existence of a direct relationship between the financial and quantitative skill of entrepreneurs and the sales and bottom lines of their companies.[3]

The sources of financial management problems that can cause business crises are diverse. Consider some of the following examples:

▶ **An industrial heating and air conditioning system installer** was losing money. Essentially, three separate businesses were operating under one roof: installation of systems, service contracts and maintenance, and sale of replacement parts. Management needed to know how each product line was performing to make decisions on pricing, staffing, or whether to divest the line entirely. Because sales, expense, and time sheet data had always been aggregated, rather than collected by business line, this information was unavailable and the company was eventually unsuccessful in designing a turnaround strategy.

▶ **A furniture manufacturer** with annual sales of $5 million was forced to write off $500,000 of receivables from customers unable or unwilling to pay. Lack of credit controls, applying payments randomly to invoices, and incomplete records all contributed to the problem. The company was forced to file for bankruptcy.

▶ **A moving company**, modestly profitable but with flat sales, failed to aggressively collect past due accounts. The company experienced write-offs that threatened to wipe out the accrued profit and suffered a surprise cash squeeze. Operations were hastily slashed to conserve cash and, because the company was an S corporation, where profits are taxable to the stockholders, the owner ended up without the cash to pay a $50,000 personal income tax obligation.

▶ **A jewelry manufacturer** suffered with a manual order entry system that was redundant and paper-laden. Seven separate forms were used to track orders, beginning with the receipt of the order, to issuing a production order, to shipping, and finally to invoicing. Five people set up individualized files, procedures, and double checks as the paper worked its way through the office and plant. In addition to the costs of redundancy, the process was costly in terms of lost orders, poor customer service, and an inability to track historical information for management.

Sometimes these types of management problems can lead to one of the most critical problems a business can face—running out of cash. Joe Namath once said he never lost a football game; he just ran out of time on a few occasions. Similarly, entrepreneurs often blame their demise on simply not having enough cash. Unfortunately, this is usually just a symptom. The problem may be failing to anticipate a crisis, waiting too long to take action, or taking the wrong action.

No matter how good a company's employees, products, or services, strong financial management is a critical ingredient for success.

Turnaround expert C. Charles Bahr had this to say:

Although the famous 'bottom line' is our agreed upon measuring stick, financial difficulties are usually the result of other ignored warning signs rather than the cause of them.

But in troubled businesses, we observe the top executive has marginal numbers skills and won't admit it. He lacks personal grasp of the numbers and their meaning in his own business. He may claim that his understanding of the numbers is 'good enough' when in fact it is not good enough. This leaves him at the mercy of the skills and diligence of others. It is [like an airplane pilot with] iced-up windows and disabled instruments. It is remotely possible to 'talk down' a blinded pilot, but the expected outcome, shall we say, is likely to be sub-optimal.

Numbers are just a means of communication, projection, and planning. In troubled companies, we see a lot of numbers, but they are too complex, too simple, mismatched to the requirements or just ignored. And they are nearly always late. Indeed, I don't believe you have to be a financial wizard to run a company today. ... I just want a CEO to understand basic addition and subtraction and to do it.[4]

Controllership

Unexciting and underestimated, the controller's role is more important than you may think. Avoiding and steering through problems like those mentioned above is the joint task of manager and controller. If a business owner or CEO is a company's navigator, the controller provides the dashboard or instrument panel. Yet, time after time, companies drift because these two key players fail to address vital financial and control issues. Why? From the perspective of a business owner, two related reasons are apparent.

Unexciting and underestimated, the controller's role is more important than you may think.

▶ First, smaller businesses usually owe their initial success and growth to entrepreneurs' skill in producing a product, delivering a service, or selling. However, these entrepreneurs usually do not have commensurate experience, skill, or interest in financial management and administration. Though finance is, arguably, the most common route to the top in large companies, few smaller business owners have such backgrounds. They find financial management tedious and are happy to leave the details to their accountants and concentrate on sales, production, or product development.

▶ Second, and more important, business owners can underestimate the scope and potential contribution of sound financial management. Financial management is often thought of in a very narrow sense, perhaps not much more than basic bookkeeping. Little is demanded of the accounting department beyond paying and collecting bills, producing regular financial statements, and filing tax returns.

Just as most businesspeople today have no trouble distinguishing between sales and marketing, it is beneficial to understand that controllership is distinct from accounting.

This narrow perception of the controller's responsibilities falls well short of the mark. Just as most businesspeople today have no trouble distinguishing between sales and marketing, it is beneficial to understand that controllership is distinct from accounting. True, controllership encompasses basic accounting, but it also includes:

▶ Management accounting

▶ Cash planning and management

▶ Credit and collections

▶ Inventory management and control

▶ Planning and budgeting

▶ Expense reduction

▶ Internal controls

▶ Information systems

In a smaller company, if limited resources preclude having two top financial managers, a controller may also handle financing and treasury functions, which in larger organizations would be reserved for the chief financial officer (CFO). Controllers also frequently handle a variety of administrative functions, such as payroll, and may also be responsible for tax work.

In addition to underestimating the scope of the controller's job, business owners and CEOs also underestimate the job's potential impact. Accounting is often viewed as a necessary evil, an overhead function, whose costs should be minimized. It may even be seen as constricting if paperwork or other procedures interfere with managers' day-to-day freedom of action. As a result, rather than investing in information systems, controls, or planning, companies run in more informal, even haphazard, styles.